C000228454

life after scandal

by Robin Soans

hampsteadtheatre and Drum Theatre Plymouth gratefully acknowledge the support of

hampsteadtheatre and Drum Theatre Plymouth present

Life After Scandal
by Robin Soans

Cast (in alphabetical order)

Lord Charles Brocket / Craig Murray / David Leigh **Bruce Alexander**
Jonathan Aitken **Philip Bretherton**
Duncan Roy / Major Charles Ingram **Simon Coates**
Edwina Currie / Diana Ingram / Margaret Cook / Sonal **Geraldine Fitzgerald**
Neil Hamilton / James Herring / Menaji **Michael Mears**
Lord Edward Montagu **Tim Preece**
Christine Hamilton / Melissa / Louise **Caroline Quentin**
All other parts played by the cast

Creative Team

Director **Anthony Clark**
Designer **Patrick Connellan**
Lighting Designer **James Farncombe**
Sound Designer **Marcus Christensen**
Video Designer **Sophie Phillips**
Costume Supervisor **Greg Dunn**
Live Music arranged by **Felix Cross**
Assistant Director **Melisande Cook**
Casting **Siobhan Bracke**

Company Stage Manager **Elaine De Saulles**
Deputy Stage Manager **Lucy Harkness**
Assistant Stage Manager **Ruthie Philip-Smith**
Set built by **Object Construction**
Additional scenery by **TR2, Theatre Royal Plymouth Production Centre**

For **hampstead**theatre:
Production Manager **Tom Albu**
Chief Electrician **Kim O'Donoghue**
Deputy Chief Electrician
Sherry Coenen
Technical Manager **David Tuff**
Deputy Technical Manager
Jonathan Goldstone
Press Officer **Becky Sayer**
(020 7449 4151)

For Drum Theatre Plymouth:
Production Manager **David Miller**
Drum Technician **Matt Hoyle**
Wardrobe Mistress **Cheryl Hill**
Press Officer **Anne-Marie Clark**
(01752 230 479)

Press Representation for Robin Soans
Kate Morley (0797 046 5648)

hampsteadtheatre and Drum Theatre Plymouth would like to thank:
Julian Hurst Carpets Ltd (020 3115 1073)

Life After Scandal was first performed at Hampstead Theatre on 20 September 2007, and previously in a shortened version for Radio 4 on 3 August 2007.

Biographies

Robin Soans
Writer

Robin Soans has, as an actor, appeared in over eighty plays, including work at the National Theatre, Royal Court, Royal Shakespeare Company, Hampstead Theatre, Tricycle Theatre, The Bush, Young Vic, and The Globe. He has made thirty television appearances, and been in twelve films, the latest two being **Pierrepoint** and **The Queen**. He played the lead role of George Loveless in Bill Douglas' epic film **Comrades** about the Tolpuddle Martyrs; and leading theatre roles include: Pinchwife in **The Country Wife** (RSC); Corvino in **Volpone** (National Theatre); Holofernes in Trevor Nunn's production of **Love's Labours Lost** (National Theatre); Alderman Wiseacres in **The London Cuckolds** (National Theatre); **Etta Jenks, Three Birds Alighting on a Field, Stargazy Pie and Sauerkraut, Shopping and Fucking, Push Up,** and **Waiting Room Germany** (Royal Court).

As a playwright credits include: **Bet Noir** (Young Vic); **Sinners and Saints** (The Croydon Warehouse); **Will and Testament** (The Oval House).
In 1997 he wrote his first verbatim play **Across the Divide**, followed in 2000 by **A State Affair** for Out-of-Joint, which went on two national tours, and appeared twice at Soho Theatre. His third verbatim play was **The Arab Israeli Cookbook**, which had a production at The Gate Theatre and a revival at the Tricycle Theatre the following year; since when it has been recorded for the B.B.C. World Service, and had productions in America, Japan, and Holland. The fourth verbatim play, **Talking to Terrorists,** was jointly commissioned by Out of Joint and the Royal Court. That was subsequently recorded for Radio 3, and has had productions in America and Dublin.
He is currently engaged in the Long Project at LAMDA which will hopefully result in a play called **Breaking Barriers in Burnley**.

Cast

Bruce Alexander
Lord Charles Brocket / Craig Murray / David Leigh

Theatre includes: **The Reporter, The History Boys, The Mandate, A Fair Quarrel** (National Theatre); **All's Well That Ends Well, The Duchess of Malfi, Three Sisters, Cymbeline, Twelfth Night, The Taming of the Shrew, Dead Monkey, Troilus and Cressida, As You Like It, The Merry Wives of Windsor, Waste, Mother Courage, Volpone, The Dillen, Henry VIII, The Time of Your Life** (RSC); **The Permanent Way** (Out-of-Joint); **Pericles** (Lyric Hammersmith); **The Beggar's Opera** (Orange Tree); **King Lear** (Globe); **The Tempest** (Almeida); **Darwin in Malibu** (Birmingham Repertory Theatre); **Pravda** (Birmingham Repertory Theatre/Chichester Festival Theatre); **Sergeant Ola and his Followers, Not Quite Jerusalem** (Royal Court); **A Midsummer Night's Dream, The Tempest, Macbeth** (ACTER on US Tours); **The Brothers Karamazov** (Fortune); **Fanshen, The Ragged Trousered Philanthropists, Optimistic Thrust** (Joint Stock); **Raymond Carver Short Stories** (Arcola).
Television includes: **A Touch of Frost, Heartbeat, The Regicides, Midsomer Murders, The Innocents, The Thing About Vince, Berkeley Square, Beyond Fear, McLibel, Dangerfield, Asylum War, Chandler & Co,**

Message For Posterity, Stick With Me Kid, Murder In Mind, The Brittas Empire, Peak Practice, Head Over Heels, Growing Pains, Full Stretch, Boon, Poirot, Thatcher: The Last Days, Keeping Up Appearances, That Week In Jerusalem, The Network, South of the Border, This Is David Lander, Juliet Bravo, Elizabeth Alone, Tiny Revolutions, No Excuses, The Price.

Film includes: **Churchill at War** (to be released), **A Christmas Carol, Dead, Ladybird Ladybird, Nostradamus, Century, Bye Bye Baby, The Long Good Friday, Giro City.**

Philip Bretherton
Jonathan Aitken

Recent theatre includes: **Who's Afraid of Virginia Woolf?, Six Degrees of Separation** (Manchester Royal Exchange); **An Ideal Husband, Present Laughter, Blithe Spirit** (Theatr Clwyd); **Skylight** (Stephen Joseph Theatre, Scarborough); **Saint Joan** (Birmingham Repertory Theatre); **Private Lives** (Glasgow Citizens Theatre); **The Importance of Being Earnest** (Theatr Clwyd/ Birmingham Repertory Theatre/Toronto).

Television includes: **As Time Goes By** (9 series), **Footballers' Wives** (2 series), **Coronation Street, Casualty, Inspector Morse, Sherlock Holmes, New Tricks.**

Film includes: **Cry Freedom, Dark Floors** (to be released 2008).

Simon Coates
Duncan Roy / Major Charles Ingram

Theatre includes: **Hand in Hand** (Hampstead Theatre); **The Constant Wife** (Gate Theatre, Dublin/Spoleto Festival, Charleston USA); **Translations, Black Snow, The Resistible Rise of Arturo Ui, Pygmalion, A Midsummer Night's Dream, Arcadia, Macbeth,**

Murmuring Judges (National Theatre); **Coriolanus, The Merry Wives of Windsor, Love Play, Luminosity, The Taming of the Shrew, The Comedy of Errors** (RSC); **Arcadia** (Bristol Old Vic/ Birmingham Repertory Theatre); **The Miser** (Chichester Festival Theatre); **As You Like It** (Cheek by Jowl – Olivier Award Nomination for Best Supporting Actor, New York Drama Desk Award Nomination for Outstanding Featured Actor); **Vassa** (The Gate); **Sinderby** (The Mermaid Theatre); **You Never Can Tell** (Thorndike Theatre); **The Importance of Being Earnest** (National tour); **Pravda, Melchester, Rosencrantz and Guildenstern Are Dead, Cabaret** (Salisbury Playhouse); **An Italian Straw Hat, Tomfoolery, A Midsummer Night's Dream, Anyone Can Whistle** (Everyman Theatre, Cheltenham); **Twelfth Night** (Northcott Theatre, Exeter); **Mr Cinders** (Theatre Royal York); **Dinner on Broadway** (Nottingham Playhouse); **Bells Are Ringing** (Greenwich Theatre); **Fiddler on the Roof** (Wolsey Theatre Ipswich); **Sinderby** (The Swan, Worcester).

Television includes: **EastEnders, The Amazing Mrs Pritchard, Dream Team, The Bill, A Touch of Frost.**

Film includes: **Beginner's Luck, I'm Not Going.**

Geraldine Fitzgerald
Edwina Currie / Diana Ingram / Margaret Cook / Sonal

Theatre includes: **Dancing at Lughnasa** (Lyric Belfast); **Mamma Mia** (World tour/West End); **We Happy Few** (Malvern Theatre); **Les Liaisons Dangereuses** (Vienna's English Speaking Theatre); **The Rise and Fall of Little Voice** (Bury St. Edmunds, Exeter); **Picasso's Women** (Assembly Rooms, Edinburgh); **The Lady in the Van** (The Queen's); **A View from the Bridge** (Sheffield Crucible); **An Ideal**

Husband (Theatre Royal Haymarket); Into The Woods, The Sound of Music, Guys and Dolls, The Cripple Of Inishmaan, An Ideal Husband (Leicester Haymarket); **Playhouse Creatures** (The Sphinx); **Sunsets and Glories, Wild Oats, Proposals** (West Yorkshire Playhouse); **Absolute Hell, The Merry Wives of Windsor, Johnny on a Spot, Napoli Milionaria, Long Day's Journey Into Night, Bartholomew Fair** (National Theatre); **They Shoot Horses Don't They, Sarcophagus, Lynchville, Worlds Apart, The Rover, Flight** (RSC); **The Rain Gathering** (Traverse Theatre); **Cinderella** (Stratford East); **Saki** (The Gate); **A Night in Old Peking, Dracula** (Lyric Hammersmith); **Steaming** (Comedy Theatre); **The Real Inspector Hound** (Young Vic/tour); **Rocky Horror Show** (European tour). Television includes: **Crossroads, Chalk, Virtuoso, The Bill, Soldier Soldier, Under the Moon, The Bill.** Film includes: **I Could Read The Sky, Romeo Thinks Again.** Radio: Numerous broadcasts including a year with the BBC Radio Drama Company

Michael Mears
Neil Hamilton / James Herring / Menaji

Theatre includes: **Osama the Hero** (Hampstead Theatre); **The Tempest** (Queen's Theatre, Hornchurch); **Measure for Measure, You Never Can Tell** (Peter Hall Company/Bath, Theatre Royal/Stratford/Garrick Theatre, London); **Hamlet, Jubilee, Comedy Of Errors, Clockwork Orange, Epicene** (RSC); **Someone Who'll Watch Over Me** (Manchester Library Theatre); **Twelfth Night, The Hypochondriac** (Octagon Theatre, Bolton); **Kind Hearts and Coronets** (Queen's Theatre, Hornchurch); **Saint Joan** (Birmingham Repertory Theatre); **The Goodbye Girl** (Albery Theatre, London); **The Odd Couple** (York Theatre Royal); **Conversations With My Father** (Old Vic); **Oliver!** (Belgrade Theatre, Coventry). Television includes: **The Colour Of Magic** (to be screened next year), **Sharpe's Rifles** (three series), **Marie Lloyd, My Family, Mary and Jesus, The Seventh Scroll, The Old Curiosity Shop, The Lenny Henry Show – Delbert Wilkins** (two series), **Inspector Morse, The Bill.** Film includes: **Four Weddings & A Funeral, Queen of Hearts, Little Dorrit, As You Like It, The Oxford Murders, Sylvia.** Writing includes: **Tomorrow We Do The Sky, Soup** (solo plays written and performed at Traverse, Edinburgh; Lyric Studio, Hammersmith; and broadcast on BBC Radio 4. Winner of Fringe First Award, Best Actor nomination at Edinburgh Festival); **A Slight Tilt To The Left, Slow Train To Woking, Uncle Happy, Jam, Arnold Darwin's Feeling Better** (written and performed for BBC Radio 4).

Tim Preece
Lord Edward Montagu

Theatre includes: **Baal** (Phoenix); **Maxibules** (Queens Theatre); **Doctors of Philosophy, Cockade** (Arts Theatre); **The Master Builder** (National Theatre); **The Mystery Plays** (York); **The Seagull** (Watford); **Little Malcolm and his Struggle Against the Eunuchs** (Garrick Theatre); **Misalliance, The Birthday Party, Mrs Warren's Profession** (CTC); **K. D. Dufford Hears K. D. Dufford** (LAMDA); **Hail Scrawdyke** (Booth, New York); **The Government Inspector** (Compass); **Much Ado About Nothing** (Ludlow); **Otherwise Engaged** (Guildford); **Cause Célèbre** (Lyric Hammersmith); **Hamlet/ Antipodes** (The Globe); **A Doll's House** (Southwark Playhouse). Television includes: **Sword of Honour,**

Kilvert's Dairy, Shadowlands, Diane, Doctor Who, The Bagthorpe Saga, Funny Farm, Forgotten Voyage, Porterhouse Blue, Growing Rich, Nice Work, Take Me Home, The Law Lord, Money for Nothing, The Planet, Against All Odds, Midsomer Murders, The Fall and Rise of Reginald Perrin, Just William, Waiting for God, McLibel, Attachments, Rescue Me, Kiss Me Kate, People Like Us, Porlock Calling Rockall, Uncle Silas, Peep Show, The Day London Blew Up, Prime Suspect 7, Margaret, The Robinsons, Fingersmith, Mrs Beeton, Foyles War. Recent films: **Bathory, Vanity Fair, Elizabeth: The Golden Age.** He presented **Landshapes**, a documentary series about the British landscape, and has written two plays for television, **Father's Day**, and **The Combination**.

Caroline Quentin
Christine Hamilton / Melissa / Louise

Theatre includes: **The London Cuckolds, Roots** (National Theatre); **The Seagull** (The Lillian Bayliss/tour); **Our Country's Good, The Live Bed Show** (Garrick Theatre); **Low Level Panic, Sugar and Spice** (Royal Court); **Les Miserables** (Barbican/Palace Theatres); **An Evening with Gary Lineker** (West End); **A Game of Love and Chance** (National Theatre/ Cambridge Theatre); **Les Enfants du Paradis** (tour); **Lysistrata** (in London and Athens); **Mirandolina** (Lyric Hammersmith).
Television includes: **Blue Murder, Life Begins, Footprints in the Snow, Von Trapped, The Innocent, Hot Money, Goodbye Mr Steadman, Blood Strangers, Men Behaving Badly, Jonathan Creek, Kiss Me Kate, Upline, Bouncing Back, Videostars, This Is David Lander, Have I Got News For You?, Whose** Line Is It Anyway?, Mr Bean, Once In a Lifetime, All or Nothing At All, An Evening With Gary Lineker, The Missing Pages, Fry and Laurie.

Creative Team

Anthony Clark
Director

Anthony Clark joined Hampstead Theatre as Artistic Director in 2003. His directing work for Hampstead Theatre includes: **My Best Friend** by Tamsin Oglesby, **Tender** by Abi Morgan, **The Maths Tutor** by Clare McIntyre, **Revelations** by Stephen Lowe, **When the Night Begins** by Hanif Kureishi, **Osama the Hero** by Dennis Kelly, **A Single Act** by Jane Bodie, **Nathan The Wise** by Lessing/ Kemp, **The Schuman Plan** by Tim Luscombe, **The Glass Room** by Ryan Craig, **Taking Care Of Baby** by Dennis Kelly. As Artistic Director for Contact Theatre his productions include: **Romeo and Juliet, A Midsummer Night's Dream, The Duchess of Malfi, Blood Wedding** (M.E.N Best Production Award), **Mother Courage and Her Children, Oedipus Rex, To Kill a Mockingbird** (M.E.N Best Production Award), **The Power of Darkness , Two Wheeled Tricycle, Face Value, Green, Homeland, McAlpine's Fusiliers.** As Associate Director of Birmingham Repertory Theatre productions include: **Macbeth, Julius Caesar, The Atheist's Tragedy** (TMA Best Director Award), **The Seagull, Of Mice and Men, The Threepenny Opera, Saturday Sunday Monday, The Grapes of Wrath, The Playboy of the Western World, Pygmalion, Saint Joan, The Entertainer** and **David Lodge's Home Truths.** As Associate Artistic Director he was responsible for the launch and programming of The Door, dedicated exclusively to the development, production and promotion of new playwriting. His productions in The Door included: **Playing by the Rules, Nervous Women, Rough and Down Red Lane, Paddy Irishman, Paddy Englishman, and Paddy...?, All That Trouble That We Had and The Slight Witch, Silence, Belonging.** Other credits include: **Dr Faustus** (Young Vic); **The Red Balloon** (Bristol Old Vic/National Theatre – TMA Best Show for Young People); **The Snowman** (Leicester Haymarket); **Mother Courage and Her Children, The Day After Tomorrow** (National Theatre); **The Wood Demon** (Playhouse, West End); **Krindlekrax** (Nottingham Playhouse); **Love Play, Edward III** (RSC). Writing credits include: **Hand It to Them, Wake** and a translation of Tolstoy's **The Power of Darkness** (Orange Tree Theatre); **Tide Mark** (RSC, Thought Crimes Festival); **Green** (Contact Theatre); **A Matter of Life and Death** (National Theatre).

Patrick Connellan
Designer

Theatre includes: **Nathan The Wise, When The Night Begins** (Hampstead Theatre); **Osama The Hero/A Single Act** (double bill at Hampstead Theatre); **Taking Care of Baby, The Maths Tutor, My Best Friend** (Hampstead Theatre/Birmingham Repertory Theatre); **Blame** (York Theatre Royal/Sphinx); **Abigail's Party** (New Vic Theatre, Stoke. Also directed by Patrick); **Into The Woods** (Derby Playhouse – nominated for TMA Best Musical Award); **Broken Glass** (Bolton Octagon/York Theatre Royal); **The Bat, A Woman Of No Importance** (New Vic Theatre, Stoke); **The Resistible Rise of Arturo Ui, Road** (Mercury Theatre Colchester); **I Have Been Here Before** (Watford Palace); **Twelfth Night, Little Malcolm And His Struggle Against The Eunuchs**

(Bolton Octagon); **Popcorn** (Bolton Octagon – A Manchester Evening News award winner. Also directed by Patrick); **This Lime Tree Bower** (Belgrade Theatre/Edinburgh Festival. Also directed by Patrick); **The Slight Witch** (National Theatre/Birmingham Repertory Theatre); **Edward III** (RSC/ Gielgud Theatre); **Paddy Irishman, Paddy Englishman and Paddy...?** (Tricycle/Birmingham Repertory Theatre); **A Passionate Woman** (Comedy Theatre); **Misery** (Criterion Theatre).

James Farncombe
Lighting Designer

Theatre includes: **Taking Care of Baby, Blonde Bombshells of 1943, Nathan the Wise, Osama the Hero, A Single Act, The Maths Tutor** (Hampstead Theatre); **Three Sisters, The Maths Tutor, Forward** (Birmingham Repertory Theatre); **Blest Be The Tie, What's In The Cat** (Royal Court); **Crooked, I Like Mine With a Kiss** (Bush Theatre); **I Have Been Here Before, Beautiful Thing** (Nottingham Playhouse); **Blues for Mr Charlie, Called to Account, Playboy of the West Indies** (Tricycle); **We That Are Left** (Watford Palace); **Vincent in Brixton, A Funny Thing Happened on the Way to the Forum** (New Wolsey, Ipswich); **Improbable Fiction, Touch Wood, Making Waves, Soap** (Stephen Joseph Theatre, Scarborough); **Dead Funny, Abigail's Party** (York Theatre Royal); **Sing Yer Heart Out for the Lads, Lord Of The Flies, The Twits, Bloodtide** (Pilot Theatre Company); **Accidental Death Of An Anarchist, A View From The Bridge, What the Butler Saw, The Hypochondriac, Dead Funny, Popcorn** (The Octagon, Bolton); **To Kill A Mockingbird, Master Harold and The Boys, West Side Story, Death Of A Salesman, Peter Pan, The Witches, Plague Of Innocence, Unsuitable Girls**

(Leicester Haymarket Theatre); **High Heel Parrotfish, Urban Afro Saxons, Funny Black Women On The Edge** (Stratford East); **This Lime Tree Bower** (The Belgrade, Coventry); **Hysteria** (Exeter Northcott); **Amy's View** (Salisbury Playhouse/Royal Theatre, Northampton); **Hang Lenny Pope, Street Trilogy** (Theatre Absolute); **Cloudburst** (Theatre Absolute, New York) **The Blue Room, The Elephant Man** (Worcester Swan Theatre); **East Is East, A Women Of No Importance** (New Vic Theatre, Stoke); **Goldilocks** (Lyric Hammersmith); **Krapp's Last Tape, A Different Way Home, A Visit From Miss Prothero, The Kiss, A Who's Who of Flapland** (Lakeside, Nottingham); **Private Fears in Public Places, Speed-the-Plow, A Day In The Death Of Joe Egg, The Price, Larkin With Women** (Manchester Library Theatre).

Full credits and production photos at http://web.mac.com/jamesfarncombe

Marcus Christensen
Sound Designer

Theatre includes as Associate Sound Designer: **Measure for Measure** (Peter Hall, Bath); **Waiting For Godot** (New Ambassadors); **Amy's View** (Garrick); **Old Times** (Brighton Theatre Royal/tour/Bath Theatre Royal); **Journey's End** (New Ambassadors); **What The Butler Saw** (Criterion); **The Hound of the Baskervilles** (Mercury Theatre/National tour). As Sound Designer: **Private Lives, Dangerous Obsession, The Rivals** (Bath Theatre Royal/tour); **The Promise, She Stoops To Conquer, Death of a Salesman, Small Miracle, Miss Julie, Blue Sky State, Devils Advocate, A Midsummer Nights' Dream, Of Mice and Men, The Resistible Rise of Arturo Ui, The Seagull** (Mercury Theatre). As Production Sound Engineer: **The Schuman Plan, What The Butler Saw** (Hampstead Theatre); **Journey's End** (New Ambassadors/

tour); **See How They Run** (Duchess Theatre/tour); **Love Songs** (New Ambassadors); **Take Flight** (Menier Chocolate Factory); **...And Then There Were None** (Gielgud); **A Voyage Round My Father, Honour** (Wyndhams); **National Anthems, The Philadelphia Story, All About My Mother** (Old Vic).

Sophie Phillips
Video Designer

Theatre includes: **Hamlet** (York Theatre Royal – York Prize Winner, Speculative Design Project); **Day Return** (Left Luggage Theatre, Realised Performance, Nottingham); **Bestiary** (Design and Publicity, Buxton Fringe Festival); **The Visit** (Speculative Design Project, West Yorkshire Playhouse); **Pillowman** (Lighting Assistant & Puppeteer, ITV Six Play Festival, Nottingham); **Once in a Lifetime** (Work Placement, Painter, National Theatre); **Six Degrees of Separation** (Work Placement, Props, Royal Exchange Theatre, Manchester).

Melisande Cook
Assistant Director

Theatre includes as a Director: **A Midsummer Night's Dream** (Jesus College Cambridge); **A Christmas Carol** (Southwark Playhouse); **Telltales** (Theatre 503) and several Hampstead Theatre Start Night and youth productions. She has been shortlisted for the JMK, C4, and OSBTTA young director's awards. As an actor: **Carver** (Arcola); **Taming of the Shrew** (UK tour); **Macbeth** (UK tour); **Boudicca** (Eastern Angles); **Les Liasons Dangereuses** (RADA); **Love's Labours Lost** (Drill Hall); **Tempest** (Graeae). As an improviser, Mel has developed and toured shows from Chicago to Auckland via Glastonbury, and has also improvised repeatedly on reality TV. She is currently devising work for the Frost Fair at Shakespeare's Globe.

hampsteadtheatre is one of the UK's leading new writing venues housed in a magnificent purpose-built state-of-the-art theatre – a company that is fast approaching its fiftieth year of operation.

hampsteadtheatre has a mission: to find, develop, and produce new plays to the highest possible standards, for as many people as we can encourage to see them. Its work is both national and international in its scope and ambition.

hampsteadtheatre exists to take risks and to discover the talent of the future. New writing is our passion. We consistently create the best conditions for writers to flourish and are rewarded with diverse, award-winning and far-reaching plays.

The list of playwrights who had their early work produced at **hampstead**theatre who are now filling theatres all over the country and beyond include Mike Leigh, Michael Frayn, Brian Friel, Terry Johnson, Hanif Kureishi, Simon Block, Abi Morgan, Rona Munro, Tamsin Oglesby, Harold Pinter, Philip Ridley, Shelagh Stephenson, debbie tucker green, Crispin Whittell and Roy Williams. The careers of actors Jude Law, Alison Steadman, Jane Horrocks and Rufus Sewell were launched at **hampstead**theatre.

Each year the theatre invites the most exciting writers around to write for us. At least half of these playwrights will be emerging writers who are just hitting their stride – writers who we believe are on the brink of establishing themselves as important new voices. We also ask mid-career and mature playwrights to write for us on topics they are burning to explore.

The success of **hampstead**theatre is yours to support

Since opening our stunning award-winning building, we have presented nineteen world premieres and twenty-one London premieres. We have commissioned forty-two writers, transferred two plays to the West End and sent twelve on national tours, and six of our playwrights have won prestigious Most Promising Playwright awards. We also have one of the most extensive education and participation programmes of all theatres in London.

Our artistic achievements have inspired increasing critical and commercial success. This has been made possible by the many individuals, trusts and companies that have already chosen to invest in our creativity. To secure our bright future we need your support.

If you would like more information about supporting **hampstead**theatre and helping us to nurture the new talents and audiences of the future, please email development@hampsteadtheatre.com or call Tamzin Robertson on 020 7449 4171.

hampsteadtheatre would like to thank the following for their support:

Abbey Charitable Trust; Acacia Charitable Trust; Anglo American; Arimathea Charitable Trust; Arts & Business; Awards for All; The Alchemy Foundation; Auerbach Trust Charity; Bank Leumi; BBC Children in Need; Bennetts Associates; Big Lottery Fund; Blick Rothenberg; Bridge House Estates Trust Fund; Swiss Cottage Area Partnership; Community Fund; The John S Cohen Foundation; Coutts Charitable Trust; D'Oyly Carte Charitable Trust; The Dorset Foundation; The Eranda Foundation; The Ernest Cook Trust; European Association of Jewish Culture; Garrick Charitable Trust; Gerald Ronson Foundation; The Goldsmiths Company; The Hampstead & Highgate Express; Help a London Child; Harold Hyam Wingate Foundation; The Jack Petchey Foundation; Jacobs Charitable Trust; John Lyon's Charitable Trust; Lloyds TSB Foundation for England and Wales; Kennedy Leigh Charitable Trust; Local Network Fund; Mackintosh Foundation; Markson Pianos; Marriot Hotel, Regents Park; Milly Apthorp Charitable Trust; The Mirianog Trust; The Morel Trust: The Noël Coward Foundation; Notes Productions Ltd; Ocado; The Ormonde & Mildred Duveen Trust; Parkheath Estates: The Paul Hamlyn Foundation: The Rayne Foundation; Reed Elsevier; Richard Grand Foundation; Richard Reeves Foundation; Royal Victoria Hall Foundation; Samuel French; The Shoresh Foundation; Sir John Cass' Foundation; Society for Theatre Research; Solomon Taylor Shaw: Sweet and Maxwell; Karl Sydow; Towry Law; The Vintners' Company; World Jewish Relief; Charles Wolfson Foundation.

hampsteadtheatre would also like to thank Mrs Jean Hardwicke for the generous donation of five Max Beerbohm prints.

hampsteadtheatre is incredibly grateful to everyone who has supported us through our Luminaries scheme over the past year:

Production Syndicate
Lloyd & Sarah Dorfman

Level 5
Elizabeth & Daniel Peltz

Level 4
Leonard Eppel CBE &
   Barbara Eppel
Sir Richard Eyre
Sir Clement & Lady Jill Freud
Arnold Fulton
Ewan McGregor
Midge & Simon Palley
Richard Peskin
Wendy & Peter Phillips
Paul Rayden
Anthony Simmonds
The Peter Wolff Theatre Trust

Level 3
Pauline & Daniel Auerbach
Dorothy & John Brook
The Sidney & Elizabeth
   Corob Foundation
David Cohen
Professor & Mrs C J Dickinson
David Dutton
George & Rosamund
   Fokschaner
Michael Frayn
Jacqueline & Michael Gee
Rachele & John Harrison
Michael & Morven Heller
J Leon & Company Ltd
David & Wendy Meller
Brian & Hilary Pomeroy
Michael & Livia Prior
Sue & Anthony Rosner
Sir David Scholey
Judy Williams

Level 2
Jenny Abramsky CBE
Bob Ainscow
Anonymous
Lesley Bennett
The Ben-Levi Family
Judith & Shmuel Ben-Tovim
Karen Brown & John Blake
Bob & Jenni Buhr

Deborah Buzan
Jessica & Shimon Cohen
Robyn Durie
Bernard Faber
Frankie de Freitas
Robert & Elizabeth Freeman
Susan & Jeremy Freeman
Jacqueline & Jonathan
   Gestetner
Richard Gladstone
Anthony Goldstein
Conway Van Gelder Grant Ltd
Philip & Nori Graham
P & F Hackworth
Elaine & Peter Hallgarten
Robin & Inge Hyman
Paul Jenkins
Harold Joels
Norman & Doreen Joels
Patricia Karet
Tony Klug & Joanne Edelman
David Lanch
Alasdair Liddell
Paul & Paula Marber
Julia & Julian Markson
Myra & Alec Marmot
Tom & Karen Mautner
Judith Mishon
Sandy & David Montague
Edna & Jerrold Moser
Nicholas Murphy
Trevor Phillips
Clare Rich
Rita & Anthony Rose
The Rubin Foundation
Marcus & Andrea Sarner
Barry Serjent
Dr Michael Spiro
Revd Derek & Mrs Estelle
   Spottiswoode
Clive Swift
Talbot Designs
Christopher Wade
Tom Wedgwood
Hugh Whitemore & Rohan
   McCullouch
Adrian Whiteson
Della Worms & Fred Worms
   OBE

Level 1
Anonymous
David Adams
Lord Archer
Regina Aukin
Graham & Michelle Barber
Eric & Jean Beecham
Arline Blass
Alan Brodie Representation
Leonard Bull
Geraldine Caulfield
John & Judith Cohen
Suzy Korel Casting
June Cowan
Mr & Mrs Michael David
David & Jose Dent
Ralph & Muriel Emanuel
Eva & Desmond Feldman
Richard Foster
Bobbie Ginswick
Mitchell Gitin
Desmond Goch
G C Goldman
Linda Goldman
Paul Harris
Anna Katz
Lady Keegan
Siegi & Valerie Mandelbaum
David & Sandra Max
Raymond Mellor
Roger & Bridget Myddelton
Thomas Neumark
Rafe & Stacey Offer
Tamara & Michael Rabin
Claudia Rosoux
Peter Roth QC
Michael & Luba Selzer
Lady Solti
Bonnie Tabatznik
Tim Watson
Denise Winton
Cecilia Wong
Anna C Young

capital campaign supporters

hampsteadtheatre would like to thank the following donors who kindly contributed to the Capital Campaign, enabling us to build our fantastic new home:

Mr Robert Adams
Mr Robert Ainscow
Mrs Farah Alaghband
Mr W Aldwinckle
Mr Mark Allison
Anonymous
Mrs Klari Atkin
Mr William Atkins
Mr and Mrs Daniel and Pauline
  Auerbach
Mr David Aukin
Sir Alan Ayckbourn
Mr George Bailey
Mr Christopher Beard
Mr Eric Beecham
Mrs Lucy Ben-Levi
Mr Alan Bennett
Mr and Mrs Rab Bennetts
Mr Roger Berlind
Ms Vicky Biles
Mr Michael Blakemore
Mr Simon Block
Mr A Bloomfield
Mr John Bolton
Mr Peter Borender
Mr and Mrs Rob and Colleen
  Brand
Mr Matthew Broadbent
Mr Alan Brodie
Dr John and Dorothy Brook
Mr Leonard Bull
Mr and Mrs Paul and Ossie Burger
Ms Kathy Burke
Mr O Burstin
Ms Deborah Buzan
Mr Charles Caplin
Sir Trevor and Susan Chinn
Mr Martin Cliff
Mr Michael Codron
Mr and Mrs Denis Cohen
Dr David Cohen
Mr David Cornwell
Mr and Mrs Sidney and Elizabeth
  Corob
Mr and Mrs John Crosfield
Miss Nicci Crowther
Ms Hilary Dane
Mr and Mrs Ralph Davidson
Mr and Mrs Gerald Davidson
Mrs Deborah Davis
Mr Edwin Davison
Mr David Day
Ms Frankie de Freitas
Mr and Mrs David and Jose Dent
Professor Christopher and
  Elizabeth Dickinson
Sir Harry Djanogly

Ms Lindsay Duncan
Mr David Dutton
Mrs Myrtle Ellenbogen
Mr Michael Elwyn
Mr Tom Erhardt
Sir Richard Eyre
Mr Peter Falk
Ms Nina Finburgh
Mr and Mrs George and
  Rosamund Fokschaner
Ms Lisa Forrell
Mr N Forsyth
Mr Freddie Fox
Mr Michael Frayn
Mr Norman Freed
Mr Conrad Freedman
Mr and Mrs Robert and Elizabeth
  Freeman
Mr and Mrs Jeremy and Susan
  Freeman
Mr and Mrs Brian Friel
Mr Arnold Fulton
Mr and Mrs Michael and
  Jacqueline Gee
Mr and Mrs Jonathan and
  Jacqueline Gestetner
Mr Desmond Goch
Mr Anthony Goldstein
Mr Andrew Goodman
Ms Niki Gorick
Mrs Katerina Gould
Lord and Lady Grabiner
Mr and Mrs Jonathan Green
Mr and Mrs David Green
Mrs Susan Green
Mr Nicholas Greenstone
Mr Michael Gross
Mr and Mrs Paul Hackworth
Dr Peter and Elaine Hallgarten
Miss Susan Hampshire
Mr Christopher Hampton
Mr Laurence Harbottle
Sir David Hare
Lady Pamela Harlech
Mr Paul Harris
Mr John Harrison
Mr Howard Harrison
Mr Jonathan Harvey
Sir Maurice Hatter
Mr Marc Hauer
Dr Samuel Hauer
Mr and Mrs Michael and Morven
  Heller
Mr Philip Hobbs
Mr and Mrs Robin and Inge
  Hyman
Mr Nicolas Hytner

Ms Phoebe Isaacs
Mr Michael Israel
Professor Howard and Sandra
  Jacobs
Mr and Mrs Max Jacobs
Dr C Kaplanis
Mrs Patricia Karet
Baroness Helena Kennedy
Mrs Ann Kieran
Mr Jeremy King
Mr Peter Knight
Sir Eddie Kulukundis
Ms Belinda Lang
Mr and Mrs Edward Lee
Mrs Janette Lesser
Lady Diane Lever
Mr Daniel Levy
Mr Peter Levy
Sir Sydney and Lady Lipworth
Mrs Alyssa Lovegrove
Ms Sue MacGregor
Mr S Magee
Mr Fouad Malouf
Mr and Mrs Lee Manning
Mr and Mrs Thomas and Karen
  Mautner
Mr and Mrs David and Sandra
  Max
Mrs June McCall
Mr John McFadden
Mr Ewan McGregor
Mr and Mrs David Meller
Mr Raymond Mellor
Mr Anthony Minghella
Mr and Mrs David Mirvish
Mr and Mrs Mark Mishon
Mr and Mrs Edward and Diana
  Mocatta
Mr and Mrs Gary Monnickendam
Mrs and Mrs David and Sandra
  Montague
Mr Peter Morris
Mr and Mrs Ian Morrison
Mr Andrew Morton
Lady Sara Morton
Mr Gabriel Moss QC
Mr and Mrs Terence Mugliston
Mr and Mrs Roger and Bridget
  Myddelton
Mr Stewart Nash
Mr James Nederlander
Mr John Newbigin
Sir Trevor Nunn
Mr T Owen
Mr and Mrs Simon and Midge
  Palley
Mr Barrie Pearson

Mr Daniel Peltz
The Honorable Elizabeth Peltz
Mr Richard Peskin
Mr Gary Phillips
Mr Trevor Phillips
Mrs Gillian Phillips
Mr and Mrs Peter and Wendy Phillips
Mr Paul Phillips
Mr Tim Pigott-Smith
Mr Alan Plater
Mr Michael Platt
Mr and Mrs Brian and Hilary Pomeroy
Mr and Mrs Michael and Tamara Rabin
Mr D Randall
Mrs Janet Rapp
Mr and Mrs Paul and Claire Rayden
Mr Robert Reilly
Mr Dominic Ricketts
Mr Gillespie Robertson
Mr and Mrs Edward Roche
Mr D Rogers
Mr Gerald Ronson and Dame Gail Ronson DBE
Mr Benjamin Rose
Mr and Mrs Anthony and Sue Rosner
Mr Vernon Rosoux
Mrs Patricia Rothman
Mr Robert Rubin
Mr Michael Rudman
Mrs Esther Rudolf
Mrs Coral Samuel
Mr and Mrs Marcus and Andrea Sarner
Sir David and Lady Scholey
Mr James Barrington Serjent
Ms Louisa Service
Mr Cyril Shack
Mr and Mrs Peter Shalson
Mr and Mrs Gerry and Sue Sharp
Mr and Mrs Mike Sherwood
Mr Richard Shuttleworth
Mr and Mrs Jonathan and Lucy Silver
Mr and Mrs Anthony and Beverley Silverstone
Mr and Mrs Michael Simmons

Mr and Mrs Mark Simpson
Mr and Mrs Michael and Zsuzsi Slowe
Mr and Mrs Jeremy Smouha
Mr David Soskin
Dr Michael Spiro
Mr Nicholas Springer
Mr and Mrs Peter Sprinz
Mr Simon Stapely
Miss Imelda Staunton
Mr Bruce Steinberg and Ashley Dartnell
Ms Shelagh Stephenson
Mr Jonathan Stone
Sir Tom Stoppard
Mr David Tabatznik
Mr Paul Taiano
Mrs Valentine Thomas
Mr and Mrs Simon Tindall
Mr Fred Topliffe
Ms Jenny Topper
Mr and Mrs Barry Townsley
Mr Christopher Wade
Mr Vincent Wang
Mr Tom Webster
Mr Timothy West
Mrs L Westbury
Dr Adrian Whiteson
Mrs Judy Williams
Mr James Williams
Mr Richard Wilson
Mr Geoffrey Wilson
Mr Peter Wolff
Lady Ruth Wolfson
Mr and Mrs Fred and Della Worms
Mrs Marion Yass
Mr and Mrs Jeffrey and Fenella Young
Allied Irish Bank
Buro Four Project Services
Casarotto Ramsay and Associates
Charles Caplin & Co
Conway van Gelder Ltd
Ernest R Shaw Insurance Brokers
Friends of Theatre
Garfield Weston Foundation
Ham & Highgate Express
Hampstead Hill School
Hampstead Wells & Campden Trust
J Leon & Company Ltd

John Lyon's Charity
Kleinwort Benson Charitable Trust
Mercers' Company Charitable Trust
N M Rothschild & Sons Ltd
Nyman Libson Paul
Peters Fraser & Dunlop
RAC Plc
Richard Grand Foundation
Samuel French Ltd
The Acacia Charitable Trust
The Agency
The Allen Foundation for the Arts
The Andor Charitable Trust
The Archie Sherman Charitable Trust
The Arthur Andersen Foundation
The Barnett & Sylvia Shine No 2 Charitable Trust
The British Land Company PLC
The Coutts Charitable Trust
The Dent Charitable Trust
The Dorset Foundation
The Drue Heinz Trust
The Duveen Trust
The Equity Trust Fund
The Esmee Fairbairn Foundation
The Follett Trust
The Garrick Charitable Trust
The Harold Hyam Wingate Foundation
The Hollick Family Trust
The John S Cohen Foundation
The Mackintosh Foundation
The Maurice Hatter Foundation
The Monument Trust
The Noel Coward Foundation
The Presidents Club
The Rayne Foundation
The Rose Foundation
The Royal Victoria Hall Foundation
The Sidney & Elizabeth Corob Charitable Trust
The Steel Charitable Trust
The Trusthouse Charitable Foundation
The Ury Trust
The Weinstock Fund
Wild Rose Trust

hampsteadtheatre would also like to thank the many generous donors who we are unable to list individually.

creative learning at **hampstead**theatre
widening access to new playwriting

Changing Lives

Our Creative Learning programme is a thriving part of **hampstead**theatre's work. We aim to celebrate all aspects of the creative process in ways which support learning and widen access to the theatre's programme. At its best, our work has the power to change lives.

> **'My first encounter with Hampstead Theatre was a primary school trip when I was 8 years old. I am now a Peer Ambassador, which involves teaching and assisting drama projects for a range of different age groups. The experience has really boosted my confidence and has made me value responsibility.'**
> (Youth Theatre Member since 2003)

We work closely with **hampstead**theatre artists and writers to find innovative ways to inspire creativity and develop emerging talent. The programme helps people of all ages to develop personal, social and communication skills. We actively engage with some of the most disadvantaged groups in our local community.

Schools Audiences – Follow Spot

We're offering a limited number of £6 tickets for Excellence In Cities schools in Greater London (available to groups attending mid week matinees and designated performances only). All other schools tickets are £10, with one free ticket for every ten paid.
Our schools audience programme makes a visit to see a show at **hampstead**theatre more meaningful, accessible and educational. Follow Spot offers exciting creative strategies for delivering the curriculum, exploring the creative practice behind a production, and increasing understanding of the creative industries. We provide:

- Free online teacher resources, including complete schemes of work for GCSE and A Level
- Free play texts (when making a booking)
- Free post show Q&A with the company and creative team
- Teacher trainings with director or writer (subject to availability) – £5 per teacher
- Bespoke pre- or post-visit workshops

'An inspiration!' 'A real refreshment of skills and ideas.' 'Excellent techniques that I can translate into my own work.'
(Teachers attending training in June 2007)

Call our Schools Tickets Co-ordinator on 020 7722 9301 to book.

Boosting Learning

At the heart of the programme is a network of long term relationships with teachers and young people at local schools. Through in-school workshops, theatre visits and youth theatre referrals, we help to improve learning, motivation and self esteem. Our script and story writing projects, for example, offer new, drama-based ways to improve literacy, which in turn boosts learning across all subjects in the curriculum.

'The programme that our school has created in collaboration with Hampstead Theatre and the Royal Court is extensive and is absolutely key to the success of the department, both in terms of exam results and also the wider and less easily evaluated development of students creativity and self worth.'
(Head Of Drama, local secondary school, March 2007)

Act, Write And More With Our Youth Theatre

The **heat&light** Company is made up of budding performers, writers, directors, stage managers and technicians aged 11 to 25. Each term four groups come together to explore the power and potential of theatre in ways which reflect the artistic practice at Hampstead. This year our groups have worked with nine writers, including John Donnelly, Nick Grosso and Steve Waters, as well as John Kani and the **Nothing But The Truth** company. **hampstead**theatre's Youth Theatre is free to all participants and produces twelve performances a year. If you would like to find out more please email **creativelearning@hampsteadtheatre.com**

'The first Heat and Light term was really good because it felt like there were no rules and you could write, act or do anything you wanted, with the freedom to perform and produce fresh and new ideas. The Daring Pairings project in which I co-wrote and produced a short play with Roy Williams was particularly enjoyable. I am now writing and acting for Channel 4's new show Skins.'
(Youth Theatre Member since 2003)

Upwards And Onwards

We aim to offer a wide range of opportunities to people of all ages. Here are some of the ways you can get involved at **hampstead**theatre, and stay with us, and move on. To find out more, email us at creativelearning@ hampsteadtheatre.com.

First contact – where you are	First visit to Hampstead	Project at Hampstead	Training & Progression
			Join Our Creative Direction Team (11+)
		Act, Write And More With Youth Theatre (11+)	Work Experience And Voluntary Placements (14+)
	See Your Play Performed By Professionals (5+)	Act, Write And More With Summer University (14+)	Develop Professional Skills (Teachers & Practitioners)
Scriptwriting And Story writing In Schools (5+)	Audition To Act, Write, More With Youth Theatre (11+)	Develop Your Play For Start Night / Daring Pairings (11+)	
Scriptwriting In The Community (8+)	See A Main House Show & Meet The Company (11+)		
Submit A Play To Start Night or Daring Pairings (11+)			

Creative Learning by Numbers

In the year April 06 – March 07 our outcomes included:
- 11,000 participants, of which 58% from a BME background, at 595 events
- 75 complete projects delivered at the theatre and out in school and community settings
- 83 educational performances in the Michael Frayn Space

hampsteadtheatre staff and company

Directors
Jenny Abramsky CBE (Chair)
David Adams FCA
Larry Billett
Paul Jenkins
Amanda Jones
Daniel Peltz
Michael Pennington
Paul Rayden
Greg Ripley-Duggan
Jeremy Sandelson

Company Secretary
Christopher Beard FCA

Advisory Council
Sir Trevor Chinn CVO
Michael Codron CBE
Lindsay Duncan
Michael Frayn
Sir Eddie Kulukundis OBE
Peter Phillips OBE
Patricia Rothman

Artistic Director
Anthony Clark

Executive Director
Bryan Savery

Literary
Associate Director (Literary) Frances Poet
Literary & Creative Learning Assistant
Katy Silverton

Pearson Writer in Residence
Alexis Zegerman
Channel 4 Resident Director
Noah Birksted-Breen

Administration
General Manager Neil Morris
Financial Controller Christopher Beard
Finance Officer Adam Halliday
Assistant to the Directorate and Associate
Producer (Daring Pairings) Davina Shah

Creative Learning
Creative Learning Director Eric Dupin
Schools Practitioner Debra Glazer
Literary & Creative Learning Assistant
Katy Silverton

Marketing
Marketing Manager Rebecca Daker
Marketing Officer Vicky Brown
Press Officer Becky Sayer

Marketing Consultants makesthree
Marketing & Promotion
(anyone@makesthree.org)

Development
Development Director Sarah Coop
Development Manager Tamzin Robertson
Development Assistant Jon Opie
Events Manager Lucy French

Production
Production Manager Tom Albu
Chief Electrician Kim O'Donoghue
Deputy Chief Electrician Sherry Coenen
Technical Manager David Tuff
Deputy Technical Manager
Jonathan Goldstone
Technician (Michael Frayn Space)
Cressida Klaces

Box Office
Box Office Manager Chris Todd
Deputy Box Office Manager
Caitriona Donaldson
Senior Box Office Assistant
Lee Maxwell Simpson
Box Office Casuals Clare Betney,
Maria Ferran, Paula Gray, Seamus Hewison,
Kate Hewitt, Colin Knight, Helen Matthews,
Oliver Meek, Holly Mills, Asha Ramaswamy,
Chris Tester, Lois Tucker.

Front of House
Front of House & Bar Manager David Scarr
Deputy Front of House Manager
Virginia Aparicio
Duty Managers Joanna Deakin,
Joanne Wilde, Sian Thomas
FOH Staff Gwenllian Ash, Adam Baker,
Sam Bailey, Katy Bateman, Anna Bennett,
Tracey Button, Geraldine Caulfield,
Amelia Cavallo, Will Church,
Florencia Cordeu, Shane Craig,
Max Davis, Ben Groener, Lindsey Crow,
Alex Jenkinson, Isaac Jones, Daniel Kent,
Rose Lewenstein, Lise Marker,
Alistair Murden, Louisa Norman,
Sarah Page, Asha Ramaswamy, Holly Reiss,
Adam Sibbald.
Head Cleaner Isabel Ramos
Cleaners Rachael Marks, Amina-O-Owusu

DRUM THEATRE

PLYMOUTH THEATRES

The Drum Theatre is an exceptional venue in the South West, consolidating a reputation both locally and throughout the UK, for producing high-risk and entertaining plays. Pioneering new forms of stage writing, physical theatre and other, innovative cutting-edge work, the Drum, as part of the Theatre Royal Plymouth complex, has taken a leading role in an ongoing national exploration of different ways of producing and seeing theatre.

At the forefront of the development of new and exciting theatre partnerships, the Drum has collaborated with several leading touring companies including Frantic Assembly, Paines Plough, ATC and Suspect Culture, as well as co-producing with theatre partners such as the Tron in Glasgow, the Traverse in Edinburgh, the Royal Court, the Lyric Hammersmith and Hampstead Theatre.

The Drum's programme is augmented with weekly residencies from, amongst others, Gecko, Graeae, Tim Crouch, Told By An Idiot and Hoipolloi. The Theatre Royal's Young Company and People's Company also have residency at the Drum and perform there at least three times a year.

The Theatre Royal Plymouth complex is made up of the Theatre Royal itself and the Drum Theatre, as well as TR2, a new, innovative and award-winning Production and Education Centre housing the theatre-making processes, rehearsal facilities and extensive education, access and development activities.

PLYMOUTH THEATRES

Recent productions and co-productions:

July 2004 — **The Owl Service** adapted by Anita Sullivan and David Prescott from the novel by Alan Garner
Producer: Drum Theatre Plymouth

September 2004 — **The Wonderful World of Dissocia** by Anthony Neilson
Producers: Drum Theatre Plymouth, Edinburgh International Festival, Tron Theatre Glasgow

October 2004 — **Through A Cloud** by Jack Shepherd
Producers: Drum Theatre Plymouth and Birmingham REP

February 2005 — **Mercury Fur** by Philip Ridley
Producers: Drum Theatre Plymouth and Paines Plough

May 2005 — **Stoning Mary** by Debbie Tucker Green
Producers: Drum Theatre Plymouth and Royal Court

September 2005 — **A Brief History of Helen of Troy** by Mark Shultz
Producers: Drum Theatre Plymouth and ATC

October 2005 — **Presence** by Doug Lucie
Producer: Drum Theatre Plymouth

February 2006 — **The Escapologist** by Simon Bent
Producers: Drum Theatre Plymouth, Suspect Culture and Tramway

May 2006 — **NHS – The Musical!** by Nick Stimson and Jimmy Jewell
Producer: Drum Theatre Plymouth

September 2006 — **pool (no water)** by Mark Ravenhill
Producers: Drum Theatre Plymouth, Frantic Assembly and Lyric Hammersmith

October 2006 — **Long Time Dead** by Rona Munro
Producers: Drum Theatre Plymouth and Paines Plough

February 2007 — **Bad Jazz** by Robert Farquhar
Producers: Drum Theatre Plymouth and ATC

May 2007 — **Speed Death of the Radiant Child** by Chris Goode
Producer: Drum Theatre Plymouth

September 2007 — **Stockholm** by Bryony Lavery
Producers: Drum Theatre Plymouth and Frantic Assembly

October 2007 — **Life After Scandal** by Robin Soans
Producers: Drum Theatre Plymouth and Hampstead Theatre

Marriott.
LONDON REGENTS PAR

Wine & dine for £25.00
in the Mediterrano Restaurant

Here's a really tasty offer. Enjoy a 3 course dinner and a glass of house wine 0.175ml for just £25.00 in The Mediterrano Restaurant. How could you resist?

Robin Soans

LIFE AFTER SCANDAL

For Christine M and Sue Z

OBERON BOOKS
LONDON

First published in 2007 by Oberon Books Ltd
521 Caledonian Road, London N7 9RH
Tel: 020 7607 3637 / Fax: 020 7607 3629
email: info@oberonbooks.com
www.oberonbooks.com

A catalogue record for this book is available from the British
Library.

Cover design by www.n9design.com

ISBN: 1 84002 805 X / 978-1-84002-805-8

Printed in Great Britain by Antony Rowe Ltd, Chippenham.

Characters

MELISSA

MAJOR CHARLES INGRAM

EDWINA CURRIE

NEIL HAMILTON

JONATHAN AITKEN

LORD CHARLES BROCKET

LORD EDWARD MONTAGU

DUNCAN ROY

MENAJI

CHRISTINE HAMILTON

CRAIG MURRAY

DIANA INGRAM

SONAL

LOUISE

JAMES HERRING

MARGARET COOK

DAVID LEIGH

and

Son, Gail, Barman, Elizabeth, Big Issue Salesman, Brazilian woman, Shop Assistant, Bouncer, Anna, Floor Manager, Cassandra, Maggie, Minnie, Muscat and various Waiters.

ACKNOWLEDGEMENTS

I would like to thank...

All at Catherine Bailey Limited for their help and support in helping fund this project and producing the radio version for the BBC. Special thanks to Catherine Bailey and Marilyn Imrie.

Hilary Norrish, who directed the radio version, for the continuing encouragement, help and advice.

My hard-working, underpaid, and dedicated research team – Jesse Quinones, Alexis Hood, and Phil Ormrod.

Matthew Parris for wise guidance.

And, of course, all the contributors for their generous and courageous agreement to talk on a difficult subject.

Act One

These opening speeches are not related to the characters in the play.

ACTOR 1: I can't think why you want to write a play about scandal; all you're doing is fanning the flames.

ACTOR 2: In fact I think what you're doing is irresponsible… that's my gut instinct…you're making a bad situation worse.

ACTOR 3: It's a spoof…it must be a spoof.

ACTOR 1: I can't see what you hope to achieve.

ACTOR 3: It must be a scam.

ACTOR 5: All you're doing is feeding the media machine.

ACTOR 1: I would have thought your standard of work was above that.

ACTOR 3: Where's the hidden microphone? Where's the hidden camera?

ACTOR 4: Tabloid-fabricated scandal is flesh-eating and disgusting. Best not to dignify it by going anywhere near it.

ACTOR 1: Don't think you're going to put a stop to it…there's only one way to put a stop to it, and that's stop buying the papers.

ACTOR 4: Do you buy a paper? You do. There you are you see. Stop it. Stop reading the papers. I did. It's amazingly liberating.

ACTOR 3: No…that's all in the past. Thank you but no.

ACTOR 4: Sorry, but no.

ACTOR 2: No way. I don't want to swill in that mire.

ACTOR 6: No, I'm not going to talk about it, no.

ACTOR 1: No, not for me.

ACTOR 5: No.

ACTOR 7: No.

ACTOR 6: No.

ACTOR 7: Absolutely not.

ACTOR 1: No!

ACTOR 5: I have to say no. It was some years ago, it was an aberration, and I've put it behind me now.

MELISSA: You see, I'd really rather forgotten about all this… I'm not sure whether I want to take part in anything which is going to start it all up again.

WAITER: Would you like anything else?

MELISSA: Just a mint tea would be lovely thanks, and you couldn't bring her the tail end of the meat from those people next door could you? She'd so love it. Isn't this the best restaurant?

I've always subscribed to the view that to say nothing is better. If you're ending a relationship, the only way to end it is not to engage. If you look at the detail of scandal, it seems to me that you're engaging.

My name is… What shall we call me? …Melissa; and I'm the daughter…let's just say the daughter. I don't want to say more than that. I'm feeling really peculiar about the whole thing. You won't finger me will you? I want to remain anonymous.

I love this place…they're not in the least interested in me, it's only my dog they love. When I came back from Portugal, I used to sit outside, and then when winter came, I left her outside, and they opened the door and said 'Prego Cassandra', and insisted she came inside. (*Waves.*) Oh look…my godmother…

I don't think it's a good idea to write a play about scandal, the only thing you'll get people talking about is scandal. I don't even know who Abi Titmuss is. Who is she?

The WAITER brings a mint tea and a bowl of food.

WAITER: Mint tea. (*Puts bowl on floor.*) And for Senora Cassandra.

MELISSA: Brilliant. One more favour, you wouldn't give me one of your cigarettes would you…I've left mine at home.

WAITER: Of course.

MELISSA: You are so kind. Thank you.

The WAITER lights the cigarette and goes.

You watch this, she'll spit the beans out, all over the floor, it'll be so embarrassing.

On the other hand, I might be wrong. No, on the other hand, if you can persuade people to talk to you it might be fascinating.

CHARLES: I may talk to you. I'll talk to you as long as I don't have to go anywhere, and it's not going to cost me any money.

EDWINA: Alright, I'll meet you in the Atrium next Tuesday at twelve o'clock...it's opposite the Houses of Parliament. I'm on air at two o'clock, but that should give us two hours. I'll talk about salmonella, but I'm not going to talk about John Major. I'll leave it to you to do the booking.

NEIL: We'll meet you outside the church in Covent Garden, after our TV interview. We'll be on our bikes. We cycle everywhere these days. I'll leave Christine to fine tune the details, I'm hopeless at arrangements...that's one of the reasons I got married.

AITKEN: Why don't you come to supper on Sunday...it'll be something fairly basic...smoked salmon and scrambled eggs I expect.

MELISSA: It'll be fascinating because you'll see them stuck like insects in amber. Like an Ibsen play...haunted for the rest of their lives.

BROCKET: Some people you look in the face...you can tell if they're suffering because of something like that. I couldn't help noticing every time I met Edward Montagu, this slight pain in his face. It was constantly there in his mind...what had happened.

MONTAGU: I'm going to sit here...it's slightly higher up; I can manage better. You can see Marble Arch from here in the winter, when the leaves are off the trees. It's a difficult decision for me to talk, some of it's very difficult to talk about, and this all happened fifty, over fifty years ago...it's difficult, raking up the past...but, well, you've persuaded me.

My full name is Edward John Barrington Douglas Scott Montagu...I've suffered all my life, I was teased at school for having such a long name, and I've never used it as such. My children have only got one name. My father died when I was two and a half, which is when I inherited the title of Lord Montagu.

BROCKET: My father died of a brain tumour when he was thirty-two, and I inherited the title Lord Brocket...Charles Brocket...Charlie B.

DUNCAN: Until recently, I didn't know who my father was. I found out in the end he was this Iranian guy who had ten children with different women. He died ten years ago. My name is Duncan Roy, and I am a film director, and I pretended to be a Lord. I grew up in a small house in an unmade road in Whitstable, on the edge of a council estate.

MONTAGU: The Beaulieu Estate was handed by my great-grandfather to my grandfather as a wedding present...it's been in my immediate family since 1860...gave him a couple of estates when he got married...quite sensible really; a large part of the family thought he shouldn't have done it; the elder son got rather shirty about it, as if he didn't have enough.

DUNCAN: My father died ten years ago leaving all his money to his last four children...and no, I wasn't one of them.

MONTAGU: I was the youngest person at the coronation of George VI. I was ten.

DUNCAN: When I was eleven? No, that's when my step-dad stopped sexually assaulting me. He started when I was five.

MONTAGU: As a little boy it was awe-inspiring.

DUNCAN: After the age of eleven he just assaulted me.

MONTAGU: I was escorted into the Abbey by a lot of ushers. I had a little black bag with ham sandwiches in it. You had to be seated by seven in the morning and the service lasted for hours. It was the same for everyone...everyone was desperate for a pee.

WAITER: What can I get you?

DUNCAN: You know what, I'm going to have the smoked haddock, it sounds divine, but not just yet...say in about half an hour. I'll tell you what I would love now, and that's a large glass of fizzy water with a lot of ice.

MONTAGU: Prep school was in Broadstairs. The Duke of Gloucester went there, the Duke of Kent...rather an upper-class prep school, a very good school. I was going to go to Eton, but war broke out, and I was sent to Canada for two years...near Niagara Falls...learned to ski, and found jazz...came home and went into Eton.

DUNCAN: Between the ages of seventeen and twenty-one, I lived my life as Lord Anthony Rendlesham. What people never fucking understand about my story...never, ever understand...I didn't do it to be somebody else, or to be rich or famous or any of that crap...I didn't want to be me. Later on I drank not to be me, I took drugs not to be me. When I was Lord Rendlesham, I got rid of all the baggage of being me...and that's the only time I've ever really been happy.

MONTAGU: Three years in the army, including Palestine, and then New College, Oxford, reading History.

BROCKET: Brocket Hall...at the end of the '80s, it was doing really well...the most successful Conference Centre in Europe; the number one chef in England...we were coining it in.

MONTAGU: I left before taking a degree...I wasn't sent down...I was offered a job in PR, in advertising, so I took it. There were only a few firms practising it then... hundreds now.

BROCKET: Being a bit of a car nut, I bought three or four Ferraris on the proceeds.

MONTAGU: I was promoting Bordeaux wine, but mostly it was Cadbury's Drinking Chocolate...I remember going to the catering managers at deb dances, and trying to persuade them to get the debs to drink drinking chocolate and not alcohol towards the end of their parties...save the young debs from getting killed on the way home.

BROCKET: By 1989 the Ferraris had trebled in value. The bank called me in and said, 'Look, we'll loan you five million to buy more Ferraris'...loaned me five million.

DUNCAN: The first time I told the lie it was pretty exciting. (*The WAITER brings the fizzy water.*) That's perfect, absolutely perfect. Thank you so much. It was in a club called Le Set in Paris, near the Opéra. I realised I could discard the wreckage of my grubby past in one fell swoop. I went everywhere...Paris, the South of France, America.

MONTAGU: From December '52 to May 1953, I was touring America, lecturing on stately homes; my historic family coronation robes, which had first been used at the coronation of William IV, also toured with me, which they found very impressive. I came home and wore them at the coronation of the present Queen.

Later that summer the disaster happened...I say disaster but...well, I was accused by some boy scouts of...yes, I'm trying to find the right word...of...inappropriate, yes that's the word, inappropriate behaviour. It caused a lot of...a lot of...publicity...scandal.

BROCKET: In early '91, the market stalled, no one in their right mind would touch a Ferrari with a bargepole, interest rates were at seventeen and a half per cent, suddenly five million became seven, seven and a half, ended up ten million, just in compound interest...trouble was, there was a cross guarantee...suddenly bang, if the car side of things collapsed, everything collapsed, the house, the business centre, the golf course, the whole shebang was about to go down the drain, and all because of some bloody cars, which were just a hobby anyway...it seemed ridiculous...so we sat round the kitchen table to hatch a plan, which was get a spanner, take 'em apart and store them...somewhere in outer London...and put in a claim for four, four and a half million, a year later, the bank came in, the bank said, 'It's our fault, we shouldn't have encouraged you, look, here's fifteen million, interest free for ten years', at which time I withdrew the claim. And then, a year after that, the police had a call...the kids' mum called the police...shopped me...she wasn't at all well, she had a drug problem...she phoned the police and told them the whole story.

MONTAGU: You have to remember I had my name dragged through...it wasn't just this country...it was headlines in every paper across the world. Having my name blackened like that made everything difficult. Certainly I felt the sky fell in...I felt not at all in control, I broke out in spots, all over my body, this awful thing called urticaria... No, I don't know how you spell it, it's like eczema.

DUNCAN: All the press said the same thing...they said I had funded...which is true...that I had funded my life to be a lord by using my credit card, and so they gave me the name 'Lord of the Lies'.

MONTAGU: Lord Brocket...a week before he went into prison, came down to stay in Beaulieu, with his girlfriend...and I said to him, 'Is there any way I can help you?' I tried to give him some advice as best I could...knowing what he was about to face; and he was astonished, he had no idea...no idea at all of my case.

BROCKET: I did know, but I'd never let on.

I'd obviously met Edward Montagu in the House of Lords, at cocktail parties...we're both car nuts. The older members in the House would make the odd reference, 'You know he's been inside?' My mother cited this thing about him...about the boy scouts; for me as a younger person, it didn't matter in the least. Dear old Edward Montagu...he couldn't have been kinder.

MONTAGU: After what I'd been through, I wanted to know if there was anything I could do to help.

BROCKET: He was fearful that being part of the establishment, you're going to get sat on very hard, more than would be normal. The police had recommended community service for old Charlie Boy...Edward Montagu was fearful I might get six months inside.

MONTAGU: The corruption of the lower classes, yes; saw me as behaving not quite as one should. I was aware...the first trial was in Winchester, very much on home ground...of people out to get me. The Chief Constable of Hampshire was particularly antagonistic...Colonel Lemon he was called... I think the thing was, he was offended he hadn't been included in the social round, I hadn't asked him to shoot on the estate...that's pure supposition...and then the police took away my passport, and faked an entry...said I'd been to Paris when I hadn't...it's obvious...when I was being cross-examined, they could say, 'Were you in Paris on such and such a date?', and I said, 'No', I could be shown to be a liar. The judge spotted it and that's what helped me to be acquitted on the major charge.

BROCKET: Yes...I'm probably going to have a vodka and tonic...it's just past twelve; it's drinks time. Sorry about the gap, the large picture's been sent away for cleaning. I try to blend the old and the new. The flat was converted by a friend of mine. 2,300 square feet of floor space. The chap upstairs...he's married to the Duke of Norfolk's sister...he said, 'I need a massive flat, cos when I wander around naked in the morning, I don't want to bump into people from the night before whose name I can't remember.'

DUNCAN: Oh look, there's Tom Dixon...you know, the furniture man...he knew me when I was Rendlesham. It embarrasses him now. He won't look...he won't look over. I might wave.

MONTAGU: Having been acquitted of boy scouts, a matter of weeks later I was rearrested along with two of my friends, and we were accused of...yes...airmen...and we were put on trial again. They were determined to get me. There were three of them really...Sir David Maxwell Fyfe, Home Secretary, Rayner Goddard, Lord Chief Justice, and the Head of the Metropolitan Police, Sir John Nott-Bower, who said he was going to 'rip the cover off all London's filth spots'. This was after the time of Burgess and Maclean, and

Maclean had been in the British Embassy in Washington you see, so it wasn't just British secrets he took to Moscow. I think what happened...the American secret service told Maxwell Fyfe there was a network of left-wing queers in this country that needed weeding out, and he should make a few high profile examples...'pour encourager les autres' absolutely. Talking about Maxwell Fyfe...he married Rex Harrison's sister...I think sister...there was a dinner party, and Maxwell Fyfe was holding forth about 'smashing these queers', and the Rex Harrison woman said, 'No doubt when you've done that, you're going to concentrate your efforts on a cure for the common cold.' (*Laughs.*)

BROCKET: I normally took the Tory whip in the House of Lords...I was aware of words being passed down the Tory hierarchy... 'This chap should know better.' The polls were down, even the broadsheets were saying we were the party of sleaze...Hamilton was the final straw...if Thatcher's legacy of tough government and good housekeeping was to be carried on, serious action had to be taken to clean up the image of the party...so yes, like Montagu, I thought I might go inside for six months.

SON: (*Off.*) Dad?

BROCKET: Yeah?

SON: (*Appearing with something on a plate.*) Can I eat that?

BROCKET: You can eat anything you like. (*SON goes.*)

DUNCAN: The judge at my trial only had one arm. He was called Babbington. I saw him in the Groucho Club three months after I got out of prison.

MONTAGU: This time I was sent down. I got a year's sentence, but I got two thirds off, no, one third off...is that right? April '54 to November '54... (*Mutters.*) ...April, May, June, July, August, September, October, November...eight months.

BROCKET: The judge flew at his own expense back from Barbados, just to deliver the verdict. When the hammer came down, he said, 'Seven and a half years.'

DUNCAN: Basically the judge said to the credit card companies that there was no chance of recuperation. He told me I had lived a Walter Mitty existence, and that I had been a parasite. He gave me…there were twenty-one counts of credit card fraud…he said, 'You've got all of these charges. I'm going to give you fifteen months for each of them, to run consecutively'…which would have meant going to prison for twenty-six years and three months…and then he said, 'Oh no, not consecutively, concurrently.'

BROCKET: Seven and a half years…I thought I'd misheard it…I thought I'd misheard it. The Group 4 man leading me down was totally amazed, he said, 'Who the fuck did you piss off?' Everyone was flabbergasted.

EDWINA: I was completely flabbergasted when the call didn't come. I liked him, I trusted him, we'd had an affair for four years from 1984 to March 1988. (*The WAITER appears at her side.*) Yes, I'll have the soup, and then the goat's cheese tart and tomato salad…thanks a lot.

I didn't stop it because I didn't love him anymore…not at all. He was now Chief Secretary to the Treasury, maybe heading for even higher office. People might start asking the wrong questions… 'What's a cabinet minister doing going up the stairs to a back bencher's flat?' I certainly didn't want to do anything which would damage his career, or, obviously, mine. You know we used to arrange our dates sitting on the front bench in the House of Commons, whispering to each other. We got a lot of fun out of that.

In December 1990 John was elected, I naturally expected he would put his friends into office. I sat there waiting for the phone to ring. It never did…I was very, very, very upset.

When we won the election in 1992 with a much reduced majority, a nasty bruising election, the next day I was in the gym, on a rowing machine, looking up at the banks of TV sets, watching all the appointments being made, no call…I got a call late the following day; I was summoned to Number Ten. I took the tube to Westminster Station, walked across the lights over Whitehall trying not to get killed by the traffic, walked down Downing Street, said hello to the police officer…the door opens as you arrive…what happened with Margaret Thatcher…you were ushered into a small room, and she would talk to you very informally…closer than we are now…it was always very personal, and it was like that when you got the sack as well…anyway, I found myself not in this small room, but in this large drawing room, the White Drawing Room, on a sofa opposite two men on another sofa…one was the Prime Minister, and one was Andrew Turnbull, the PM's Private Secretary. I looked at this man Turnbull and thought, 'What the blazes are you doing here?' It meant John and I couldn't have a proper conversation for a start. The Prime Minister said, 'Edwina, I'd like you to join the government, and I'd like to offer you the job of Minister of State in the Home Office.' I said, 'What does it involve?' Andrew Turnbull said, 'We want you to be Minister for Prisons.' I said, 'I've got a couple of prisons in my constituency, I know what a terrible state they're in…'

BROCKET: I remember Montagu telling me that prisons are hell…he had this medieval memory of conditions…it wasn't his memory that was medieval, it was the conditions that were medieval. He'd been inside, and anything to do with a sex offence, you're labelled a nonce; he was presumably labelled a nonce, and in those days I expect he had a bloody tough time. I know he thought that anyone remotely good looking would have a problem in the showers. (*Starts to go, and calls off.*) Oh by the way, the polo kit's arrived. (*To us.*) This sheikh's sent him a polo kit. (*Calling off.*) You've got to pay import duty on it. (*To us.*) I told him there's no such thing as a free lunch. (*Goes.*)

MONTAGU: I started off in Winchester Prison, and the day before I was moved, I was in my cell; the Warder came in and said, 'Follow me.' He led me to the Governor's office…I think I sat down…I think so…and the Governor gave me a long lecture about how I had disgraced my class and would be despised and rejected for ever…just as the working-class men of London had rejected Edward VIII,

and had spat on pub floors on hearing the abdication
speech. The next day I was moved to Wakefield Prison.

AITKEN: I had one rather naïve view... (*Opens bottle of red
wine and pours himself a glass.*) ...I misguidedly thought that
once I had pleaded guilty and got to prison, everything
would calm down. In terms of the recent past...I...every
time I thought I was getting out of the crashing building,
another piece of unexpected masonry would hit me on the
head. I was I suppose a totem pole for things left-of-centre
journalists don't like. I came from a privileged background;
I went to Eton...a hate-word for many; went to Oxford,
for some people a hate-word; I was related to a newspaper
family...Lord Beaverbrook was my uncle. They saw me
as the quintessence of everything they loathed...class,
arrogance, power...a right-wing, fascist, arms-dealer; some
sort of Mr Big with millions if not billions in the bank, and
a string of mistresses, and as such I was the recipient of an
astonishing amount of hate.

I went to prison at the start of the Silly Season, and
somehow 'What's happening to Aitken in prison?' was the
story everyone wanted. When the weather was nice, for
example, you would want to be with the agricultural side of
prison, but this was virtually impossible, um...being...er...
constantly under siege from the paparazzi.

MONTAGU: When I moved to Wakefield, I'd have much
preferred to work on the outside farm than stay inside and
make shirts, but it was considered that I would be a target
for the Press. I've always pitied the man who had to wear
the shirts I made.

GAIL: (*Entering with a cup.*) A cup of your special.

MONTAGU: That's most kind. This is Gail.

GAIL: Chauffeur, gofer. You name it. I'm just nipping to the
post office.

MONTAGU: (*Handing her a letter.*) Take this will you?

GAIL: I'll only be a couple of minutes. Is there anything else
you need?

MONTAGU: No, fine, fine, thank you. (*GAIL leaves.*) I was in a cell by myself. It was so cold...it was incredibly cold in my cell. I was sleeping with my clothes on, and it was summer too...it seemed to be more like a film than reality. I had this sensation of being detached from my body...looking down on myself...outside my cell looking down on myself...it was a release of...trying to get rid of it all, escaping from it. Sometimes it would last a few minutes, sometimes a few hours.

DUNCAN: I got this sense of floating through events...from the moment I left my body, when my step-dad assaulted me at the age of five. And it was exactly like that when I went to prison. I was in Brixton Prison for four months, and Wormwood Scrubs for six.

EDWINA: Prisons...it was going to be a contentious issue. I said, 'Thank you but no thank you. Isn't there anything else?' John Major said, 'You were not around when we tried to phone you', and I said, 'When?', and he said, 'Earlier today', and I thought, 'That's a lie', and then he said, 'You can't say "no", I've put it out in a press release.' I thought, 'You prat.' I said, 'Can I ask you something? Why couldn't you put me in office when you were first made Prime Minister?' And John Major said, 'I'd forgotten about you.' And I thought, 'You double prat.' And I thought to myself, 'One day you will remember.' There I was on that sofa, looking at someone I'd been so close to, so recently, thinking it was reasonable to expect a modicum of special consideration...Turnbull was smoking...he was smoking and smiling...he thought the interview was quite funny.

I walked out of Number Ten...I was wearing a black coat, a rather smart black coat I bought in a second-hand shop in Paris...I was wearing this black cashmere coat, and all the photographers were there, and I'm sure my ministerial car and driver were waiting to whisk me off to the Home Office, and I walked back down the pavement looking like the black widow in the advert for Scottish Widows...I re-ran the scene in my mind as it should have gone. We would have met in a small private room, just the two of us;

he would have kissed me and then said, 'There are three or four jobs still vacant, these and this and this, Edwina...do you have a preference?'...looking deep into my eyes...I would have said, 'The one which is for the country's good, which one is that?' and he would have said such and such, and we would have had a serious conversation.

I must have walked home...like the Queen I walk quite a lot...but you don't remember the walk when your brain is thinking, 'What's going on?' There had been no personal contact whatsoever between us. He hadn't a clue...hadn't a clue I was hurt; he had no idea how to persuade me to join the government; no idea how to make use of my talents... one of his best communicators; he couldn't see it was the be-all and end-all of my life to join the government and make a good job of something. The only feeling I was left with was betrayal. I felt insulted...to be told he'd forgotten about me. So crass, and it meant the only link between us was broken, and our unspoken deal no longer existed.

I had this feeling of something totally irreversible; a Rubicon had been crossed; you're reeling, and you don't know why. And that was the damage done then...at that moment. I've never regretted it...prisons...

AITKEN: Stanford Hill Prison is on the Isle of Sheppey, sort of in countryside, there are trees in the vicinity; with a modern telephoto lens that's quite near enough to get pictures...anyway there was this chap up a tree...none too carefully concealed...with his camera.

MENAJI: Here we are...it's the beast...it's a Canon...it's a tool of the trade...it's a bit of a beast. I'm a paparazzo, but I'm not telling you my name. My camera does eight and a half frames a second, it's all digital...forget film, film's great, but too much aggravation... (*To BARMAN.*) ...I'll have a beer...

BARMAN: Tiger okay?

MENAJI: Anything as long as it's not crap... (*To us.*) ...it's a 2.8 70-mil to 200-mil zoom with auto-focus...now that means you only want the one lens...that's vital, you don't want to be fucking about changing lenses in the middle of the action. You don't carry a camera bag cos then everyone knows you've got a camera...you have a bag that looks like any sort of bag...you don't have any bits with you; you won't be far from your car...you can have all your shit in the car.

For your more powerful shots, you need a tripod, but usually in that kind of situation you're in a bush, or up a tree, on the beach, or behind a wall looking onto the beach.

So this is a zoom lens, good for a low light, and you can put a doubler on this if you want to get in close. You spend a lot of time outside someone's house, we call it the location, and you have to be there early before they leave.

AITKEN: When I was living in Lord North Street, it was not odd to find photographers on the pavement at 6:30, or waiting in their cars. What they were after was today's picture of the 'beleaguered minister'. I would come out of the house, there would be a sort of convergence...a score of flashbulbs kicking off...they were after a grimace, looking gloomy...'Gloomy Aitken'...something like that. They would shout; the shouts would be straight out, and they would be a snippet of something they'd got from the *Guardian* or the *Independent* that morning, which I didn't know about... 'What about the BMARC meeting on the 15th June? Did you approve guns to Singapore? Did you procure girls for the Saudis?' Sometimes the Press Officer from Number Ten would phone to say, 'There's a story on the front page, it says such and such, I thought you should know before you go out to face the barrage.'

MELISSA: I told you. I told you she'd spit out the beans. She's carefully licked off all the gravy and spat out the beans.

Let me tell you something... I was going to the dentist, to have my...what do you call them...wisdom teeth...it was an anaesthetic, and I saw a billboard saying that my father had resigned for health reasons, so I was alarmed that he was ill. When I found out it was a sex scandal, it made me laugh because it was such a relief he wasn't ill. I came back from the dentist, and there were hundreds of press outside the house, a scrabbling throng, exactly that...I was really traumatised…it's such an incredible invasion of your privacy…people up trees, a man up a tree screaming 'How do you feel?'…outrageous…it just couldn't be more unpleasant…couldn't be more unpleasant.

Why should I tell you how I feel? I wouldn't talk to you about my sex life, it's private, and to talk about the details of that day would be prurient…

WAITER: I think she has finished, Senora Cassandra.

MELISSA: She adored it thanks. Sorry about the mess.

WAITER: No matter…we all love her, your dog. Is she what… a spaniel?

MELISSA: No, a saluki. You're fingering me. There aren't that many salukis in Holland Park.

That's why if you want to know what went on behind the curtains, and by the way we didn't have any curtains, and what I feel, or felt, is not interesting…it's private, *no but*, it's private, it's a powerful word if it's used properly. Even you discounted that word. I saw you sort of smirk. What *is* interesting is what's got a hundred and fifty people camped outside the house and up trees for nothing.

AITKEN: I was followed all the time, by journalists and photographers in cars…you can imagine how oppressive it was in the car or walking, playing cops and robbers all day long until they'd got 'today's picture'.

MENAJI: There's always paparazzi cruising in their cars, following someone as they go about. Look, look at this…I was at an actress's house, outside her house, couple of hours ago…on a scout…followed her home on the off-chance…you never know who's gonna turn up…photographed this girl who turned up…don't know who she is….could be anybody…she didn't know I was photographing her…out the window of my car…scratching her thigh look…running her hand through her hair…look at this one…checking her mobile phone. Following is always better. I went through twelve red traffic lights in a fortnight following Kate Moss…there may be other paparazzi following her...you don't want them getting 'the shot'. What you want is an exclusive. If someone's snorting cocaine or picking their nose, I'll leave that alone, but a lot of photographers are looking for that...crack-sweaty-arse-pants-zoom in on armpits, all sorts of crap. You only ambush someone if it's going to be difficult following them, or there's a back entrance out of a building and you can't cover it.

AITKEN: I did escape by a back entrance very early one day. It was five o'clock, a lovely sunny June morning. In the night I had a dream about my father...everything very disturbed...I was moving towards resignation, I was very miserable...suddenly I had the idea after waking that I might go to the Suffolk churchyard where he's buried. I looked out the window, and saw these two bulky guys, heads back, mouths open, fast asleep in their car. I couldn't risk going out the front door. In Lord North Street, my mother's flat adjoined the house; I got into her flat and slipped out the back door...got to my car without being seen, and drove out to Playford churchyard. I hadn't been for ten or fifteen years, and...um...I had a bit of trouble finding the grave...there it was. It said, 'Sir William Traven Aitken, KBE, Member of Parliament for Bury St Edmund's. Died Playford Hall, January 10th 1964.' He was a marvellous man, a real 'Knight-of-the-Shires' MP...a war hero with an impeccable record. He died of his wounds really. He'd been really badly burned and shot up; in hospital he'd had something like 142 operations, and this at a time when anaesthetics were fairly primitive; I wasn't unhinged, but I suddenly found myself sobbing and sinking to my knees on that gravestone, and saying, 'Dad, I'm so sorry, I really mucked it up, I haven't been the sort of son you wanted.' And there was above me, in that cloudless blue sky, there was a lark in full flight and singing absolutely full throttle, and Anna Airy's cottage next door with the sunlight dancing about on the roof tiles, and a lot of childhood memories came flooding back. Only a moment's respite...then it was back to the metropolitan jungle, which, as far as I was concerned, was a media jungle.

MENAJI: The ambush is when you jump out in front of them and blitz them. The cry is 'Go, go go', and we all jump out.

AITKEN: On the day we withdrew from the libel case, I was close to breaking point. I knew I was ruined, and I couldn't bear to see all those reporters glorying in their victory. On top of that, on that same day, I had to put out a press release saying that my wife and I were separating. I don't think any marriage could have survived that amount of media intrusion.

I wanted to keep my head down; I fled to New York. Yes, I suppose...yes...somewhere I could be anonymous. When I phoned home, my daughter said, 'Daddy, you're not just the news, you're the only news.' Of course I thought she was exaggerating, but then I was faxed a copy of the *Evening Standard.* The banner headline was, 'THE RUIN OF AITKEN', in that magnified type-size used for great crises or the death of royalty; further down in pretty large letters it said, 'DOWNFALL OF A FORMER CABINET MINISTER', and underneath it said, 'AITKEN, THE MARRIAGE, PAGE 3; AITKEN, THE TRIAL, PAGE 4; AITKEN, THE LIES, PAGE 5, AITKEN, THE MAN, PAGES 12 & 13; LEADER COMMENT PAGE 9'.

It was a low point, very low, very low, yeah.

CHRISTINE: I couldn't have got lower. I didn't get out of bed some days. Neil had to come into the bedroom to persuade me it was worth getting out of bed at all. I could only sleep with sedation. I didn't go to the supermarket. I didn't go out. I spent most of the time sitting in an armchair, staring ahead, just staring at the wall, motionless, staring at the floor; or just mooching about. We were right down on the floor.

NEIL: Not just on the floor...through the floor.

CHRISTINE: When the chips are down, when they're really down, you're totally on your own, even within the marriage. I'm sure it was the same for Neil.

NEIL: Your lives have been shattered in the most public way imaginable.

CHRISTINE: Drinking? Gosh yes. I'm not unaccustomed with alcohol in normal life...but then...I would just drink myself into oblivion...wine generally...or gin...it was quicker... and then just fall over.

NEIL: Subside...collapse. There was a time when there didn't seem an obvious way out.

AITKEN: I definitely thought about suicide...I had this moment...I went out for a run one morning in Northern California, in this huge wilderness on the edge of the Pacific, and there was a place where the cliff rose sharply... I looked down, and the fall was far deeper than I had imagined. I was...um...it took me by surprise. It would have been very easy to er...to er...leap off that cliff and be dead in ten seconds. This thought tempted me for a few seconds, but then I came back to my senses. I thought of my sixteen-year-old son sleeping in the log cabin, his tousled head on the pillow...I thought, 'Even if I'd like to end it all now, I couldn't possibly do it because of how tremendously selfish and cruel it would be to him and my other children.' Looking back I think that was the low point.

CHRISTINE: We plummeted straight down. On the night of the election, we went from being DINKies to NINKies, from Double Income No Kids, to No Income No Kids. (*To WAITRESS.*) I'll have a pot of the Fountain Blend please. What about you Neil?

NEIL: Earl Grey for me I think.

WAITRESS: One Fountain Blend, one Earl Grey.

NEIL: And that's with lemon please, no milk.

CHRISTINE: Something to eat...we shouldn't really...we've had two lunches today already...we've recorded two episodes of a thing called 'Destination Lunch'...we had our first lunch at ten o'clock this morning...not that we got that much to eat...so perhaps some smoked salmon sandwiches... sheer greed...one between two...thanks so much.

BROCKET: The low point for me was when I first went to prison. It really did look as if I might lose everything...

even the estate, everything. My children were on the other side of the world, their mother was a drug addict and in trouble, my brother told me one of the staff was breaking into my office at Brocket Hall on a daily basis and running off with things, and my current girlfriend who I rather naïvely thought I was going to marry…she legged it six seconds after I went inside which told me a lot about her.

MONTAGU: Yes I was…I was engaged…at the time I went into prison. I'd rather not talk about it…didn't survive of course…still very sensitive, even after all this time. My mother was very distressed.

BROCKET: I was sent down on February 12th, my birthday… on the 14th…Valentine's Day…I had expected a hundred and fifty cards from her all in one breath…she was excessive in things like that…not one card arrived. Being an intelligent chap I put two and two together. She did visit me a week later, expressed undying love, and the next day disappeared off the radar. I was pretty down. It was the shame of it. I was the one put in charge, and I was the one who had mucked up and ended up in prison.

AITKEN: So there I am in prison, with this chap up a tree with his telephoto lens, and this other guy hiding in some clumps of long grass with another long lens. It's definitely the economics of tabloid journalism that's driving this activity. Some Sunday newspapers I know only too well will easily spend sixty thousand pounds to fill up a page or two, especially if they can get a shot of me having a pee, or smoking a roll-up cigarette. The only time I got hit in prison… I was standing on the wing, and this man said, 'I'm really pissed off…my nan died last week…she brought me up as an orphan et cetera, I want to go to the funeral, and the Governor's refused permission, it's bloody unfair.' I said, 'I'm sorry, is there some way you can appeal, get him to change his mind?' And he hit me, and tearfully pulled out this newspaper, and there was this huge half page, 'AITKEN ALLOWED OUT OF GAOL TO GO TO WILLIE WHITELAW'S FUNERAL', and the report went on to say I'd had tea and cucumber sandwiches with the

Governor who'd given me special permission, and I'd gone to the funeral with two prison officers, talked to Margaret Thatcher and Lord Carrington...not one single word of it was true.

MENAJI: You won't be quoting this under my name will you? They fucking do whatever they want to do whenever they want to do it. They buy the photographs off me, and then they just make up the headlines and the captions underneath...the story underneath is nonsense. They'll quote people in a restaurant...that they were chatting happily with so-and-so, or having a row with so-and-so, and there was no one there but the photographers and them.

AITKEN: There were gains from the media attention...the prison community warmed to me because of it... 'This guy's just like the rest of us, he's fucked up his life, doing his bird, and along come all these shits from the media'...especially after the first recorded instance of someone breaking into prison. I was approached one day by a prisoner who I hadn't seen for a while...which with hindsight wasn't surprising...he'd been released the month before, and had been paid by the *Daily Mirror* to break back into prison. Three accomplices on the third floor had also been paid, five grand, to winch him up to their window. He came over to me looking very uncomfortable...he was wearing his green prison overalls, but also, rather oddly because it was a hot day...um...a black woolly hat and a bulky sort of windcheater thing, and he...um...came over to me... 'Can we go over to that tree over there?' 'Okay.' 'How's Lady Aitken?' 'Fine.' 'How are your daughers?' 'Fine.' 'Is it true Margaret Thatcher's coming to visit you soon?'...this rather mad dialogue. We went to the corner of the canteen, he didn't eat his lunch, he was behaving distinctly oddly; then he said, 'I must talk to you somewhere private, can we continue this conversation in your peter?'...that's my cell...so we headed towards my cell...by then one of the accomplices had shot his mouth off about the five grand, and the Irish boys had rumbled what was going on, and we were just reaching my cell, with this guy saying, 'Tell me about your problems', when Mickey came running down the corridor… 'Look out Jonno, this guy's a wrong 'un.' I said, 'We're all wrong 'uns in here, Mickey.' Big Jim shouted, 'He's got a camera stuffed up his front, and there are wires sticking out his back, he's wired up for sound.' The guy started to run…Big Jim unsuccessfully tried to rugby tackle him; Mickey said, 'We've got to grass him up.' We found Prison Officer Rook, who said, 'What's his description?' Mickey said, 'He's got wires sticking out.' I said, 'He's wearing a black hat.' Rook thought I said, 'He's as black as your hat', and with all the alarm bells ringing and officers pouring out of everywhere, every black prisoner in the place was put against the wall rather ferociously; meanwhile our friend was being lowered out of the third floor window with the Irish shouting, 'He's escaping, he's escaping'…and one officer, the fattest in Stanford Hill, waddled after this man who scaled the perimeter fence and sped off in a waiting car.

The spirit of the prison was entirely for me… 'Jonno, this is a bleeding liberty'…black guys thought it was a terrific joke; one of them gave me the high fives cos he had drugs on him, but the officers were so busy looking for wires sticking out, they missed the drugs.

ELIZABETH: (*Head round door.*) Jonathan?

AITKEN: Yes?

ELIZABETH: We're getting rather peckish. Are you going to be much longer?

AITKEN: I'll be with you any second.

ELIZABETH: Shall I start getting it ready?

AITKEN: On my way. I'll do the eggs. (*Getting up.*)

ELIZABETH: I'll do the toast. (*Goes.*)

AITKEN: (*Calling after her.*) Try not to be Queen Alfred. (*Back to us.*) Right at the end of my sentence, I was in the office being searched and processed after Christmas leave, and I was asked to go upstairs to see the Deputy Governor, who said, 'There's been a serious plot against you.'

BROCKET: Jack, covered in tattoos, had been an enforcer for one of the London gangs…Jack came up to me and said, 'Charlie, I've got to tell you', and he named three guys.

AITKEN: 'Three of the prisoners have been overheard making the arrangements.'

BROCKET: 'They're gonna sort you out in the showers, and then sell some photographs via the screws to the fuckin' newspapers.'

AITKEN: Apparently a well-known tabloid had offered them forty thousand quid to put a drug called Rohypnol in my tea which keeps you awake but totally immobilised.

BROCKET: I said, 'What do you mean?'

AITKEN: They were going to put me in bed naked with another naked guy, take photographs, and then run the story, 'AITKEN TURNS GAY IN PRISON'.

BROCKET: Jack said, 'Don't worry, they won't do it now. One's got a broken arm; one's got no nose, not as you'd call a nose anyway, cos I smashed it against the wall so hard there's nothing left, and the other one's legged it.' There was no more funny business in the showers.

AITKEN: There's an art to scrambled eggs…the secret is to cook them slowly… (*Going.*) …you can't hurry them. (*Out.*)

BROCKET: I got on famously with everyone in the nick because I'd spent five years in active service, where you learn to live with the men, fight with the men, and sometimes die with the men.

MONTAGU: Many of the warders were from my old regiment…I was an officer…Lieutenant eventually…and they had been non-commissioned officers, so yes, I had been their senior in the army, and now the roles were reversed…but they treated me very well. Well, we spoke the same language you see.

BROCKET: (*Going.*) If you've been in the army, you learn to talk with the men, not at them. Archer had problems in prison because he talked at people not with them. (*Out.*)

DUNCAN: I was having such a good time in Wormwood Scrubs I didn't want to leave. I could have gone...I was offered to go and laze around in an open prison, but I was, I have to admit it, having great sex in prison...with the sort of men I've always liked...sort of straight men...and I was only twenty-two and really good looking.

MONTAGU: After all the mayhem of the publicity and the two trials, prison was a sort of fixed point. I had time to study in prison...I studied Estate Management.

DUNCAN: I made my cell so nice the other prisoners wanted to come round and visit me.

MONTAGU: When I got out, nobody foresaw a recovery. My defending counsel...yes, it was defending counsel...dead now...in his summing up at my trial had said, 'You face a bitter future.'

DUNCAN: After I got out of prison, I bumped into this posh woman at the Evening Standard Christmas party...the second editor was a friend of mine...not Max Whatsisname, his second in command...she saw me across the room, and came over, glowering. She said, 'What are you doing here? Who invited you?' 'My friend.' 'Oh', she said, 'I thought we'd dealt with you.' She was outraged that I was even there. She was incensed. She just walked away.

MONTAGU: I wasn't meant to recover.

DUNCAN: Soon after that, I met this old aristocrat...he told me, 'You should just disappear.'

MONTAGU: I think I was meant to disappear.

The company sings a verse of 'Hit the Road, Jack'.

DUNCAN: This aristocrat said, 'I expected you to go and work in a nursery'... no, not a nursery...what are they called... greenhouse...'You should go and work in a greenhouse, with all the other hothouse plants.'

MONTAGU: (*Going.*) One or two people advised me to go abroad, at least for a few years. In fact a member of the family sent a business colleague to see me, and offered me a lot of money to stay abroad...he didn't want the family name dragged through the dirt.

I didn't see why I should disappear. It wasn't their intention that I should outlive the experience, but I was determined to do it. (*Out.*)

NEIL: People were clearly determined...

CHRISTINE: Oh yes, everyone was determined we were not to rise again.

NEIL: We were invited, as a kindly gesture, before the Downey Report...

CHRISTINE: After Downey...

NEIL: Before Downey...

CHRISTINE: After Downey...

NEIL: By Charles Moore, editor of the *Daily Telegraph*...

CHRISTINE: Kindly said, 'Come and have a glass...a drink with me at The Savoy.'

NEIL: We met in the American bar at The Savoy... (*Takes jacket off.*)

CHRISTINE: Fizz...jolly nice...

NEIL: His advice was go to America, go to New York, and start all over again.

CHRISTINE: It was meant to be helpful advice.

NEIL: He clearly thought I was unemployable; there was no future for me in England, go to another country without all the baggage. (*Takes bow tie off.*)

CHRISTINE: I'm sure... I know he meant it kindly.

NEIL: Staying here was like trying to get a hopeless show on the road.

CHRISTINE: Like we were sleazy, like we were corrupt. You're not going to take anything else off are you Neil? You seem to be removing clothes at an alarming rate.

NEIL: Rather warm in here. Pushing fifty, lost my seat, controversy swilling around one...no one was going to take a risk.

CHRISTINE: Neil went on 'Newsnight'...Mark Mardell threw out a question...Neil started to say, 'This isn't correct...you know it was Timbuktu actually not Melbourne'...that sort of thing...Mardell said, 'But that's just detail. No one's interested in that.' He just tarred Neil with the broad brush...'This man is corrupt, and I'm not interested in fact.'

NEIL: I could do nothing against the avalanche which was engulfing us.

The tea arrives. One WAITRESS, one WAITER. Two trays, two pots of tea, two strainers, cups, plates, milk for CHRISTINE, and a smoked salmon sandwich with half a lemon wrapped in muslin.

WAITER: Fountain blend?

CHRISTINE: For me, thanks so much.

WAITRESS: Earl Grey.

NEIL: Thank you.

WAITRESS: Lemon.

NEIL: Thank you.

CHRISTINE: What's that? Is that hot water?

WAITRESS: Yes madam.

CHRISTINE: Oh just bung it in the middle, that's fine; and just put the sandwich in the middle, that's lovely. Thanks so much.

What hope had we got with tabloid filth poured on our heads every day?

DUNCAN: Suddenly all this vitriol is pouring on you. You look me up on the Internet...con man, queer, violent, vindictive, psychopathic... This woman in one of the newspapers said people shouldn't sit down in the same restaurant as me.

CRAIG: Ever since I stood up for human rights in Uzbekistan, the British Government has been actively telling people that I'm an alcoholic, that I'm mentally unstable, and that I'm corrupt. I'm Craig Murray and I was our Ambassador in Tashkent. Almost as soon as I got there, I found I was working with an appalling regime...persecution of anyone who didn't tow the official line, show trials, huge number of executions...they don't hang people they shoot them... even people being boiled alive. The main victims of torture were Muslims and anyone who belonged to religious sects, like Hizbut Tehrir...a bit like the Moonies. The purpose of the torture was to make people confess they were members of Al Qaeda, and had links with Osama bin Laden. Because Uzbekistan was supposed to be an ally of ours and housed a strategic US airbase, I was ordered to stay 'on message' which effectively meant ignoring this violation of human rights. What I really objected to was the use of evidence obtained under torture to bolster the Foreign Office's narrative that the Uzbek regime was a bastion against Islamic militancy. But then the powers that be are convinced that the very fabric of our...of Western Society...is being threatened by a few madmen with beards, and anyone who doesn't understand that is a danger to society...QED they must be got rid of.

DUNCAN: I was being made an example of. By sending me to prison, nothing I ever said again could be taken seriously.

CRAIG: There's no doubt they set out to destroy your reputation, permanently. I've had to face the relentless hostility of a government, because of their absolute determination to remove someone objecting internally to what they were doing in the name of the War on Terror, and the most effective way to drive them out of society is scandal; is to blacken their name. The thing that really hurt were the accusations of corruption; they virtually accused me of stealing money from the Embassy. On the question of personal morality, I've never pretended to have any. But while shagging around is one thing...visas in return for sex is quite a different matter. So is stealing...these are seriously hurtful allegations.

NEIL: Suddenly you become a sort of public property for people to be moralistic and judgemental about.

CRAIG: That's what scandal does to you...you're pitched into the public arena in such a way that everyone is allowed an opinion about you, but you yourself are not allowed an opinion.

CHRISTINE: Millions of people who didn't even know you existed feel they can pass judgement on you.

DUNCAN: You become sort of dustbins into which everyone else can pile their rubbish.

NEIL: The most frustrating thing of all...people out there can hit you, and you can't hit back.

CHRISTINE: One of the things that annoyed me the most, was that every square inch of your body language is analysed. This photographer asked me to stand behind Neil and put my hands on his shoulders, and I perfectly normally just placed my hands on his shoulders as you do...this led to all sorts of psychobabble...that Neil had somehow...

NEIL: I had misbehaved.

CHRISTINE: They said...I don't know...my hands were digging in...that I...

NEIL: That I was a naughty boy, and she was a stern mummy remonstrating. 'Don't go out on your own again.'

CHRISTINE: If I wore a particular brooch to court...

NEIL: Everything is regarded as symbolic...

CHRISTINE: One day I wore a dragon brooch... 'Oh look, that's the mood she's in today.' Can't let it get to you...it does of course, cos suddenly you're persona non grata. The phone suddenly goes dead.

NEIL: No one wants to know you.

CHRISTINE: Pass by on the other side.

NEIL: I passed Michael Ancram the other day...

CHRISTINE: Great fat slob rolling out from the Beefsteak... grotesquely fat...well he is.

NEIL: The Beefsteak's at the bottom of Charing Cross Road...

CHRISTINE: One huge lunch table...politicians, lawyers, diplomats, journalists...it's an establishment club...

CRAIG: The Establishment, and whatever media they can control, close ranks, and their idea, their main aim, is that no one will ever take you seriously again.

The Establishment in this country still exists...that's top civil servants, captains of industry, the people who run BAE for instance, British Aerospace, the main political parties, the top ranks of the BBC...

NEIL: The Establishment is and always has been more interested in preserving the integrity of institutions than any notion of justice for the individual.

CRAIG: A senior presenter on the 'Today Programme', whom I'm not going to name, but you could say *the* senior presenter on the 'Today Programme', for example, told me that when I was about to appear on his programme, he had had one of these phone calls from the Foreign Office warning him against me, saying, 'You do know Craig Murray is a deluded alcoholic, don't you?'

DUNCAN: Without a single moment's doubt there exists in this country a series of string-pullers...if they can spot you as someone whose behaviour is perceived as being bad form and not towing the official line...you must be ridiculed and humiliated.

CRAIG: That's how it works. You're shut down and shut out. You become a non person. The Establishment are conducting an orchestra...that's a bad analogy actually, you can't collectively conduct an orchestra, but you know what I mean. They decide when to shed people, and when to collude I suppose; when to divert the mob's attention onto people. They're free to carry on their own scandals undetected. You become a non person.

NEIL: Totally emasculated.

DUNCAN: Or if you make them look foolish, and that's what I'd done, I'd made them look foolish...you must be taught a lesson.

NEIL: Put the stone across the vault...you have to be buried... never to be revived.

CHRISTINE: Find a lake and jump into it.

NEIL: Anyway…Michael Ancram…

CHRISTINE: Couldn't we talk about something nice?

NEIL: At the time of our case Michael Ancram was Chairman of the Tory Party. I was fighting against gargantuan odds with no support at all from Tory Central Office…quite the opposite…if I encounter him now, it's all smiles, but at the time he came out onto the steps of Central Office and effectively said, 'I hope the Hamiltons will go and bury themselves in the sand.'

CHRISTINE: 'Go and fall on your swords for the good of the party, bugger the rest of your lives.' In politics you have an enormous number of colleagues…they desert you in droves when you're on the front of every newspaper…

NEIL: In a disobliging way. Too inconvenient to be seen with.

CHRISTINE: You know the sort of thing…people who busy themselves when they see a *Big Issue* salesman up ahead… pretend to be busy on their mobile phones, so they don't have to make eye contact.

NEIL: You're treated as a squalid nuisance which needs to be removed.

CRAIG: You're meant to bury yourself, accept your exile, and vanish from the scene.

DUNCAN: We need our pariahs, so the rest of us can carry on our smug little lives with a clear conscience. It's all so fucking convenient. (*Exits.*)

CRAIG: It is a crushing experience…that's actually a very good metaphor…huge weights pressing down on you from above, which you struggle to get out from under. What was particularly depressing was the malice with which I was being pursued. It was dark…terribly dark…I got in such a state over this that I had a breakdown…I ended up in St Thomas's on suicide watch, with a large male black nurse following me into the toilet to make sure I didn't slash my wrists…you can't get much darker than that.

WAITER: Coffee and biscuits.

CRAIG: Thank you.

WAITER: Sugar's on the table.

CRAIG: Thank you. You know I'm amazed at this process…the process of how you become a non person. Let me tell you this story…the Foreign Affairs Committee, over the last two years, has interviewed…let me get this right…nine different witnesses about me, ranging from the Foreign Secretary to senior diplomats, to the heads of Human Rights Watch and Amnesty International, and they've asked them why they think I was sacked, and about the things I've been saying about torture and intelligence and Extraordinary Rendition… so I wrote to the Foreign Affairs Committee, and said, 'You have questioned all these witnesses about me and my views, would you not like to question me direct,' and I concluded, I concluded with, the end of the letter with, 'I feel I have become a non person.' And one week later I got a letter back from the Foreign Affairs Committee saying, 'Dear Mr Murray, the Foreign Affairs Committee has declined to accept receipt of your letter'… (*Laughter.*) …that's true… (*Laughter.*) …'has declined to accept receipt of your letter'.

CHRISTINE: And what people forget…the punters, the average person…and what the people who are stirring the pot don't care about…there are people at the middle of these stories, and families…there are families behind the people they're putting down.

NEIL: The pressure they're applying…the emotional damage, the psychological damage…they must know what they're doing.

Door bell. Bird song. Small dog barking.

DIANA: Down, Maggie, down.

CHARLES: Come on in, come in, there's no standing on ceremony here…I'm Charles Ingram, this is my wife Diana. I'm afraid you'll have to take us very much as you find us.

DIANA: Come here Maggie. Don't mind her, she's fine. It is a lovely house, thank you.

CHARLES: We were in Cambridge last night...Diana and I were invited back for the Freshers Debate...the motion to the house was, 'Women are better at ruling the world than men'. Diana proposed the motion, and on her team were John Sergeant, the ex-political commentator on the BBC, and Jeremy Vine. My team I felt was a bit weak...the runner-up from Miss World, 2003, Miss Canada...she went to Cambridge which is why I suppose she was there...and Kev Sutherland, a stand-up comic from Bristol...it was supposed to be Max Clifford but he didn't turn up, so it rather fell on my shoulders...my team won by a landslide... Ayes 103, Cons 333, abstentions 110. I would say this...

DIANA: He would say this...

CHARLES: My speech won the day, so rather revelling in glory, we didn't get home 'til three in the morning, still recovering really; they wined and dined us extremely well. I took my camera and told them to take some photos...it's the most simple kind of camera, but it didn't work, so there you are hey-ho. Anyway when I stood up...

DIANA: When you stood up to speak last night....

CHARLES: I got up to oppose the motion...there were five hundred in the room, and three hundred watching on monitors outside...and half the people...

DIANA: At least half...

CHARLES: Half the people erupted into coughing and clearing their throats. I said, 'We'll clear our throats, shall we, before I begin'...it got a big laugh, and that's five years on. 10th September 2001 I was in the hot seat on 'Who Wants To Be A Millionaire?'...I was a rollover contestant from the 9th...

DIANA: I was there too...

CHARLES: I went up on a Sunday for the first night...the army weren't aware at that stage...there was no reason why I shouldn't be on a quiz show...my point being, the first time

I ever informed the army was on Monday morning. I came home because I had to report for duty.

DIANA: We also didn't have anything with us.

CHARLES: Didn't have any clothes. I reported for duty at 8 AM to my line manager, my boss...he was a full colonel...

DIANA: Peter somebody...

CHARLES: His name doesn't matter. Let's leave names out of it.

DIANA: (*To dog.*) Can you not do that Maggie please...those aren't for you.

CHARLES: Any chance of another cup of tea?

DIANA: What now?

CHARLES: Thanks darling...and no it wasn't him anyway.

DIANA takes his mug and starts to exit, calling the dog at the same time.

DIANA: Come on Maggie, Maggie...Maggie...come on Maggie. (*Gone.*)

CHARLES: And I broke the good news...I had got up to eight thousand pounds on 'Who Wants To Be A Millionaire?', would they mind if I had the day off. Anyway that was fine.

I won my million pounds fair and square. The question for the million was...yes...um...what is the name given to the number one followed by a hundred noughts? The possible answers...I can't remember the exact order now...the first was googol, the second was nanomole, the third was megatron, and the fourth was gigabyte. It took me a few minutes, but specially with my physics A level, I could work it out. I knew gigabyte was a billion bytes, which is one followed by nine zeros; as far as I can remember I thought nanomole to begin with, but then I said to myself, 'Hang on, that's something tiny...the decimal point is in the wrong direction.' You've heard of a nanosecond, haven't you? I changed my mind. Celador thought this was deeply suspicious. The jury thought this was deeply suspicious. Megatron...well megabyte is a million bytes, so I assumed megatron would be a million somethings, which

would be followed by six noughts. So therefore it must be
googol...but remember, you're sitting in the hot seat, you
know you don't know the answer, you've got Chris Tarrant
spinning it out for all it's worth, and you're facing a drop of
468,000 pounds...a plummet down to 32,000 quid which is
your safety net. But of course it was the right answer. They
were convinced I wouldn't get beyond 32,000...that I was
intelligent rather than very bright...bumbling major, quote
unquote...Tim-nice-but-dim, quote unquote.

Everyone in the army was very happy, delighted for us.
All of a sudden, the children's education wasn't going to be
an issue anymore. We could pay off our credit cards, give
some money away to our friends, and there were various
charities we were keen to contribute to. But basically it
wasn't going to change anything. The army was a way of
life. I would be in until I was fifty-five, fifty-seven, and I
would have hoped...one star general or brigadier not for
me to say...but I would have hoped to become at least a
full colonel...so another fifteen or seventeen years to serve.

When it was about to be broadcast, there was a letter
on the doormat...not through the post...delivered by
courier...Major Charles Ingram on the envelope...it said,
'Due to reasons our end'... (*Puts his head in his hands.*)
...'your part in the 'Who Wants To Be A Millionaire?'
show due to be broadcast on September 18th 2001 has
been postponed.' Our immediate reaction was that it was
because of 9/11...literally the following morning after I
got the cheque in my hand the planes flew into the World
Trade Centre. I obviously concluded that it wouldn't be
suitable showing someone winning a million, big party,
and then straight into Trevor Macdonald showing the
deaths of three and a half thousand people. So we didn't
think anything of it other than, 'That's a shame.' Then
what happened? A few days after that, my wife got a phone
call from Paul Smith at Celador saying he needed to talk to
me... I tried, I did, remain reasonably calm as he informed
me that due to their suspicions of cheating, Celador had
reported the matter to the police. But how on earth do you

tell your bosses, especially in the Ministry of Defence, that you've been accused of cheating? It's horrendous, hideous, hideous. It's the people, the soldiers you lead... (*DIANA comes back in with two cups of tea and gives one to CHARLES.*) ... the mere fact of an accusation is utterly, utterly damaging, especially in an organisation like the army which is so reliant on honesty, integrity, truthfulness and the like.

DIANA: We were completely stunned, weren't we, by the whole thing. Maggie, stop it or you go out. (*She sits looking out the window, gripping her cup with both hands.*)

CHARLES: Most people in this country wanted to believe in the deception...it was the great British crime, and thoroughly entertaining, but at our expense...my, my wife's and my children's expense. We don't have a right to go into Starbucks anymore without being called a cheat.

DIANA: Vigilante justice.

CHARLES: Thirteen-year-old kids...I'll go out on a run from here...and I'll have some snotty-nosed thirteen-year-old kid coughing right in my face.

DIANA: There's a local shop down the road, and I actually have to pick my time. I never go when the local school is being let out...they all stand in the shop coughing or line up behind the baked bean tins and shout 'cheat'. They write 'cheat' on the car with dirt, with mud.

CHARLES: We've got a Volkswagen Sharan, a seven-seater, it's been car-key scratched, we get nails under the tyres regularly; the cat's been shot at with an air pistol.

DIANA: We wouldn't, we can't send our kids to the local school...they would be bullied to death.

CHARLES: (*Eating a biscuit.*) It's persecution...sheer, unabashed persecution. We're fulfilling the role of the witch in the fifteenth-century village...

DIANA: Haven't quite got a ducking stool.

CHARLES: We're constantly getting eggs thrown over the fence...

DIANA: I've had eggs thrown at me...

CHARLES: And coughing of course…always coughing. I was in India recently…I was in a street in Delhi, and two British tourists were pointing and giggling, and then started to cough.

DIANA: Ah, no…well, we can't move really…

CHARLES: I would prefer to move, albeit locally. My father lives in Warminster and my brother lives in a place called Redlynch south of Salisbury, so I want to be near them. But then there's the practical aspect…it would cost us three or four thousand…what with the deposit, and the odds and sods of actually moving…and we just don't have that sort of money. I've lost everything…from the moment I was convicted.

DIANA: We thought we might go to prison…we were told to take bags packed to court, just in case, but we got a suspended sentence…eighteen months suspended for two years each.

CHARLES: When the judge told us we had to pay 115,000 pounds, he knew we were going to be bankrupt…he knew it would be difficult for me to get a job in the near future… it's proved impossible. When my case went in front of the Army Board in August 2003, it was a bit of a rubber stamping job really…there's no way I could lead soldiers again…no way…the bond had gone. The only complaint I had with the army…they wouldn't let me talk to the media. I was never allowed to say anything but 'no comment'.

I lost my way of life…the whole package…it wasn't just my job, it was the dentistry…the dental treatment you get in the army…the school allowance…the camaraderie…not to mention my integrity.

DIANA: We have no money…we've both been made bankrupt. We've had to sell things that were precious to us / …we had to sell…

CHARLES: We had to sell the grandfather clock and the baby grand…both family heirlooms. Since August 2003 I lost the army subsidy towards the rent. It's horrendous…it's the one bill we have to pay before anything else. We're trapped…we're actually trapped. No estate agent is going to take us on… a) any house we moved into would get wrecked. We suffer at least one incident a month, and the police do absolutely nothing. And b) the estate agent will require proof of income, and neither of us have an income. So we're actually stuck here, we're almost prisoners in our own house. It's very very cold in the winter, it costs an absolute fortune to heat; and there's a vast garden which is a nightmare to keep on top of...I do all that myself. We're probably amongst the poorest and worst off in the country...I would say in the bottom 0.1 per cent...it's that bad...even some of the poorest families can drink, can smoke, can go out and cause trouble on the streets, and we can't...and they can eat.

DIANA: We have to be very careful.

CHARLES: We have severe problems eating. We wouldn't eat at all if we didn't go to Devizes market and buy the stuff at the end of the day which is the next best thing to going off.

DIANA: We eat healthily.

CHARLES: Yeah, we eat healthily, but it's not easy. No, no we can't come out to lunch.

DIANA: Oh we could, couldn't we darling? Wouldn't it be nice to...?

CHARLES: No, I've got a lot to do...a lot of writing. I must get on. It's very kind of you, but no.

The bottom line is, everybody else won with this story... the press had a field day, the public had a laugh, the solicitors and prosecutors gained kudos and press attention, Celador made a mint...the show had been plummeting down the ratings and thanks to us shot up again...when Trevor Macdonald fronted this programme called 'Major Fraud', the viewing figures peaked at 24.9 million; there were five ad breaks in that show alone and ITV made a million pounds on each one...and yes, the first ad was for cough medicine. Everyone won except us.

As I say I've just come back from India. They make us look so materialistic. There's a real appreciation of spiritual values there...they really respect individual rights...you come back here…no one cares for the individual…no one; I mean that, and it's amazingly sad.

DIANA: Our pets have been a huge source of support…Maggie the dog, and Minnie the cat.

CHARLES: They're always pleased to see you. You take a few minutes out, to go for a walk or a run, with some snivelling shit coughing at you, and trying to spit in your face…you come in and get a friendly slurp from the dog.

DIANA: Meanwhile I'm beavering away happily making jewellery.

CHARLES: And I've written a book. It's a thriller called *The Network*…it's set in the world of international terrorism. It's a condition of the interview that you have to buy two copies. I'll give you a good price…two signed copies for twenty quid. I can't say fairer than that. Twenty quid. Alright? That means we can eat.

CHARLES leads the company in a blues version of 'Brother, Can You Spare a Dime?'

BROCKET comes downstage with his drink to address the audience.

BROCKET: In the nick, I met this seventy-two-year-old Roman Catholic priest…Irish…who said to me, 'You know that bit in the Bible where it says "Vengeance is mine saith the Lord"?' and I said, 'Of course I do', and he said, 'What does it mean?', and I said, 'Well, you know, it's not for me, it's for the Lord to do something', and he said, 'No, you're wrong…it means what goes fucking round, comes fucking round. You just watch…all these people that have been on your back, sure as hell they'll fuck themselves…they'll all get their fucking come-uppance, every last one of them.' Rather amusing, all this foul language coming out of the mouth of this elderly priest. Anyway, I remember thinking, 'Here's hoping.' Cheers.

Blackout.

Act Two

The front of the stage becomes Oxford Street. A busy pavement, traffic noise. A BIG ISSUE SALESMAN is trying to attract the attention of a crowd of people in a queue for a book signing.

BIG ISSUE SELLER: *Big Issue.* Anyone else for a *Big Issue* today?

A BRAZILIAN WOMAN hurries on.

WOMAN: Is this actor arriving here?

BIG ISSUE SELLER: Someone's arriving here.

WOMAN: He plays in 'Baywatch' yah.

BIG ISSUE SELLER: Do you know him?

WOMAN: No, I don't know him. He's American.

BIG ISSUE SELLER: Anyone interested? Anyone like to say 'yes'? Anyone like to be a customer?

A SHOP ASSISTANT and a BOUNCER come on.

SHOP ASSISTANT: Downstairs. Anyone wanting anything signed you have to go downstairs.

WOMAN: Where's that?

SHOP ASSISTANT: Through the doors and then down the stairs. This is not the queue.

BOUNCER: Clear the space, clear the space.

SHOP ASSISTANT: This not the queue. You'll have to join the queue downstairs.

WOMAN: I see him. I see him. (*Runs off.*)

SHOP ASSISTANT: Through the doors. (*Runs after her.*)

BIG ISSUE SELLER: Anyone slightly interested in buying a *Big Issue*?

BOUNCER: Move that way; move that way now.

BIG ISSUE SELLER: *Issue. Issue.*

BOUNCER: Move back. Everybody move back.

An open-top bus arrives. Cheering. A lot of whooping. People take photographs on their mobile phones. Shouts of 'There he is!'

SONAL and LOUISE come on with their shopping bags.

LOUISE: We weren't planning to come today.

SONAL: No, it was spur of the moment.

LOUISE: Spur of the moment. We live in Essex; we were coming in to do some shopping, and noticed it was on. We thought it would be a gas.

SONAL: Just fun really. Look at that.

Two people run past with a standee of David Hasselhoff.

LOUISE: Cos he's a student icon…he's a real icon…the god of plastic, the god of naff.

SONAL: But clever.

LOUISE: He must be really clever…he's done all these naff things, and he's survived, and everyone knows who he is.

SONAL: We all watched…

LOUISE: Yeah, we all watched…

SONAL: Watched it laughing…

LOUISE: Thinking, 'How can he be so plastic?' But we really enjoyed it, and you sort of respect him. He's an icon of a bygone era but he's still a celebrity.

SONAL and LOUISE exit. JAMES, CRAIG and DUNCAN come in to separate tables.

DUNCAN: We're living in a celebrity epidemic. People will do anything to get a foot on the ladder, and I mean anything. I was standing in a loo queue in a Hollywood director's house…I was sandwiched between these two famous black actors…this girl came up to us and she was all over these two black guys like a rash…she totally ignored me until they said I was a director and then she was all over me as well…she said she would do anything to get to know us better. One of the black guys said, 'Anything?' and she said, 'Anything.' So he said, 'Okay. I'm waiting for a piss, I'll piss down your throat.' And in front of us all he did it, and was filmed by the other guy on his camera. How disgusting. How debauched. And yes, she swallowed it. What the fuck did she expect to achieve by doing that? It just shows the frenzied climate of celebrity we're living in.

JAMES: I want to show you some figures on the computer. I'm James Herring of Taylor Herring Public Relations. And I want to show you the calendar...just a sec... (*Goes to the door.*) ...Anna...see if you can find the Abi Titmuss calendar. Not long ago Abi Titmuss was a nurse, earning fourteen grand in an A&E ward; now she's bought a house, a car, and she's got a six-figure salary with our help. And her calendar was the biggest seller last year...it outsold Kylie Mynogue.

(*Taps keys on computer.*) Here we go...two footballers... Michael Owen...he was the golden boy of British football, clean and upright; and David Beckham. Let's see how famous they are. I've always thought the best modern indicator of fame is Google...it brings up the number of articles with their name in it. So Michael Owen...3,720,000 mentions of his name; and now David Beckham...13,600,000...and you have to understand why. David Beckham understands the rules of modern celebrity...give the media a story to entertain the readers; get a new tattoo every six months, get photographed covered in blood, go out in a sarong. Constantly reinvent yourself...this is how many new haircuts David Beckham has had in the last two years; and this is the really key one... relationships. Relationships are the most important driver of showbiz media stories. You can be a really unimportant celebrity, but if you start going out with another celebrity, your fame index shoots up dramatically. Victoria Beckham once said, 'I want to be more famous than Persil Automatic', so let's put it to the test, see if she's made it. We'll feed 'Persil Automatic' into Google and I get...2.6 million hits. Now I put 'Posh' into Google and I get 5.6 million hits...so she's achieved her objective...well done Victoria, but it's pretty impressive from Persil as well. Her own career hasn't burned as brightly as David

Beckham's…so, separately not that interesting, but together all powerful…as long as they don't lapse into being Mr and Mrs Nice. Enter Rebecca Loos…she put her hand up, said she'd had an affair with David Beckham, gave all the details to a Sunday paper, and carved out herself a career as a celebrity in her own right, thanks to the saintly Max Clifford. Rebecca Loos made an enormous difference to brand Beckham…it secured them fame and riches for at least another five years…overnight they became more human, more interesting, more real. We're all saying we're human…mucky, sweaty, warty, fallible…and now…yes, the Beckhams are just like us, we can identify with them, and follow the soap.

CRAIG: All the people who become involved in celebrity need scandal to keep their storylines going.

DUNCAN: Like the characters of 'EastEnders' their storylines have to be beefed up or they'll disappear from the public spotlight.

CRAIG: When you have no discernable talent, if you don't sleep with twelve people next week you'll drop out of the headlines.

JAMES: And that's what Fleet Street understands…pumping out the soap opera of life. Anyone who still thinks newspapers are for information has lost the plot. I mean, be honest…what would you read first…the Trade Figures for March, or a rent boy pooing on an MP? Good news is no news…bad news is great.

LOUISE and SONAL come back on.

LOUISE: Scandal…everyone likes a scandal…definitely.

SONAL: It puts a human face onto celebrity.

LOUISE: If you're watching someone famous…like Keira Knightley's got it all like…so to watch her split up with her boyfriend…

SONAL: Like the humanness of it…

LOUISE: Makes her just like us…means I can talk about her like I know her.

SONAL: Idle chit-chat…fills up the day.

LOUISE: It makes work more interesting…

SONAL: Talk about their problems. You might meet a stranger, and to talk about Keira Knightley gives you a common ground.

LOUISE: Scandal's even better cos it's like a soap, and you're all waiting for the next chapter…leaves you wanting more.

SONAL: With something like Kate Moss's coke addiction… someone comes into the shop…it gives you something in common to talk about…breaks the ice…so you can sell them something…sell them a top…cos you've got common ground.

LOUISE exits to become ANNA. SONAL sits down and transforms into MELISSA.

JAMES: Nice, sane, ordinary people aren't very interesting… either to the media or the public. The Tories…always more interesting when they're doing disgusting things, or in bed with several people at once.

MELISSA: Nowadays scandal's so easy to create. Little boys and little girls can become famous overnight by doing something disgusting on a Reality TV show.

JAMES: Reality TV has a lot to answer for. It's eight years since the first 'Big Brother' hit the mainstream. This sort of warts-and-all, up-close-and-personal, unedited kind of TV became mainstream entertainment. Nobodies became massively famous overnight. *Heat* magazine found it could sell more copies with Jade Goody on the cover than Elizabeth Hurley.

DUNCAN: More people voted for Chantelle on 'Big Brother' than voted for any politician ever…she got double the votes Tony Blair got at the election.

JAMES: It's a seismic shift…and because the public attitude has been stoked up into wanting this really mucky and sweaty side of life, this is what you have to serve up in ever increasing quantities. Mundane is the new exciting…eating disorders, cellulite, credit-card debt, divorce, parking tickets. If you can bring a celebrity together with a gritty story, you've hit the jackpot.

ANNA comes in with the Abi Titmuss calendar.

ANNA: Is this what you wanted?

JAMES: Brilliant. Thanks. Here we are...the ultimate picture... look at that. You remember the internet sex tape thing... there was a tape of Abi Titmuss and her boyfriend videoed engaged in bedroom antics, which got nicked and ended up on the internet; so see here...she's photographed sitting on a bed, with the infamous tape in the background... look...head held high... 'You're not going to kill me. I'm above all that.' It was as much therapeutic for Abi as well as making shed-loads of money out of it. She said, 'Fine, if I'm that interesting to newspapers, we're going to have a laugh about it, only this time on my terms.' Here we go look...behind the desk with a cigar... 'Abi Titmuss, chairman of her own private company Scandal Limited'. (*Goes.*)

MELISSA: Scandal is the hottest currency of the modern era. If you had a stock market with all the marketable commodities on it...gold, coffee, zinc etc...scandal would be right up there. It's a really effective way of reining in the unruly elements...the elements that threaten the power base.

DUNCAN: It's such a powerful controller. That's what nobody fucking realises.

MELISSA: You emasculate people's intelligence and their ability to discriminate by drowning them in a tidal wave of nipples and groins.

CRAIG: When you've got a media which has abandoned any ideas of education or intellectual values to determine its agenda, it opens the door to news management.

MELISSA: You do think you're going mad these days, don't you? The most ginormous scandals happen...David Kelly...and they don't get a look in.

CRAIG: When the Andijan massacre happened two years ago in Uzbekistan...the biggest massacre of demonstrators since

Tiananmen Square, it was marginalised by something trivial. If I remember right, it was Kylie Minogue's breast cancer.

MELISSA: That's what's interesting. Where's everybody's conscience gone? I was horrified, haunted as a little girl by Biafra...things like Vietnam and Biafra...now nobody gives a toss...we're all looking at some tits.

DUNCAN: It's all so convenient. While we're all watching these celebrities yo-yoing up and down you can bury any amount of bad news. Look, I've sort of dried up. I'm sorry.

CRAIG: When I was trying to interest the voters of Blackburn in torture, or the use of intelligence gained by torture, they were much more interested in who'd won 'Big Brother'. Everyone is living their lives through these iconic figures promoted by the media...and the trivia of what's happening to them.

MELISSA: It's interesting that it's scandal that's being used to manipulate people...the systematic feeding, feeding, feeding of salacious detail; not a meritocracy, or a plutocracy, but a sleazocracy. I must go; thanks for a lovely meal. Goodnight.

WAITER: Goodnight. Goodnight Senora Cassandra.

MELISSA: She adored it. I couldn't steal another of your cigarettes, could I? For the walk home; and she's got to do her business.

WAITER: Of course.

MELISSA: You're so kind. You do despair of the world now. It's almost as if you need scandal to be a rounded person, and wear it like a badge of pride. I'm really beginning to think it would be a good idea if we were all blown up. Come on Cass. Night.

MELISSA goes crossing MARAGARET COOK coming on.

CRAIG: When I published my book and the press were reviewing it, even the high-minded reviewers in the *Sunday Times*...I mean my love life occupies five per cent of the book, but that's all they concentrated on...the sex bits... and hardly at all on the issues of human rights and

torture...the political content. But that's the point...they
don't want anyone to take you or the issues you raise
seriously. It was exactly the same with the ridiculing
of Robin Cook...at the time he split from his wife and
married his secretary; it was all about the sex scandal
and nothing about the foreign policy. With such a high
proportion of divorce you wouldn't have thought it would
have caused that much of a stir. But it was still used against
him and it's because Blair and Campbell had an agenda.
Blair wanted to undermine Cook, and draw attention away
from what he was standing for.

MARGARET: In retrospect, I didn't expect it to be such a
scandal and provide such a media storm. I'm Margaret
Cook. I've been sitting outside most of the day...unheard
of in Edinburgh at the end of September...at lunchtime
it was almost too hot. Oh yes I do some water-colouring
to relax...it's a kingfisher. (*Miaow.*) That's Muscat, she's
our cat...she's a tortoiseshell and very old. We called her
Muscat because we were sitting having a bottle of Muscat
when she decided to move in. Our old cat was called
Gumpoldskirchner Neuberger...Gumpy for short...cos we
had a bottle of that when she decided to move in.

I was a consultant haematologist in Livingstone in West
Lothian, in Robin's constituency. We met at university in
Edinburgh...in the '60s...we were both members of the
Debates Committee...we met arguing across the chamber.
He was much better at debating than I was...he would
quite often wipe the floor with me. Oddly enough in a
family situation...we had a good strong family...robust...
Robin had difficulty trying to get a word in edgeways.
With our relationship, it was one of our strengths that
we did different things. I wasn't a political animal...not a
Westminster creature. I never went to Party Conference.
Robin actually was quite relieved about this...he didn't
want to be responsible for an appendage attached to him.
When it became convenient of course, it was something
different. It was ten years before...the first affair I got to
know about. She ditched him and I was expected to put

the pieces back together. I thought he was so absorbed in politics that he wasn't that sort of guy, and he wasn't what you would call classically handsome. In the ensuing ten years, he started to climb the political ladder, but there were progressive tensions in our own relationship. I wondered if I should leave him, but then our family as a whole was happy and integrated so we kind of hung on in no man's land...then of course Labour got in.

CRAIG: One of the pillars of the Labour Manifesto when they came to power was an ethical foreign policy, and at one of the very first cabinet meetings, Robin Cook tried to stop the export of BAE Hawk jets to Indonesia...because the Indonesian government, an appalling regime, uses them against the internal dissidents...they're the good guys...and he wanted to know how you could possibly square selling these jets with any notion of an ethical foreign policy. Tony Blair overruled him at Cabinet, and did it in a deliberately humiliating way...confrontational and humiliating. 'I'm the new Prime Minister, I've got a mandate. I say what happens in Cabinet. Do you want to stay or not?' Immediately after that a relentless campaign started up in the newspapers about Cook's relationship with his secretary. He'd been having an affair with her for yonks...everyone knew about it...but that was the trigger... his objection to British Aerospace Hawk jets to Indonesia, and then Campbell, probably at the behest of Blair, would phone up a newspaper and say, 'Use the stuff on Cook, he's getting a bit uppity...dig out Gaynor.'

MARGARET: Robin had only been Foreign Secretary for three months...he'd never fallen foul of the media before, never had to deal with the nasty side of things.

There we were in the VIP lounge at Heathrow...we were going off on our summer holidays...we were going to The States...Boston and then on to Montana...partly to celebrate Labour's victory in the election, and partly our surviving a rocky patch in our relationship. We were trying to let bygones be bygones. We seemed to a certain extent to have reconstructed the marriage. He turned round and told, no, shouted at everyone to get out…very rude, he could be incredibly rude…and we were left in there by ourselves, and he told me the story about Gaynor and told me it was going to be in the *News of the World*…they'd been sitting outside his flat in Sutherland Street, and found him coming out in the morning and putting money in the meter for Gaynor's car. The *News of the World* told Alastair Campbell they were going to run the story that Sunday, so Alastair Campbell phoned Robin and told him he had a day to decide what to do, which is when he told me he had to make a choice, and said, 'Sorry, we're not going on holiday, and sorry the marriage is over as well.'

I said I was not going to be dispensed with, with five minutes notice, we must talk about it, so we went back into London to his official residence, and talked for an hour over a bottle of whisky…it would have been a good one knowing him, a malt almost certainly…and at the end of the hour it was obvious he meant it.

Blair had always seen Robin's stance on morality in Foreign Policy as a threat…he and Campbell were probably rubbing their hands with glee that Robin had blotted his copybook.

CRAIG: This is using scandal to achieve your political ends. It did work. His public image was completely undermined. From then on he was portrayed as a lecher, characterised that way with great success by Rory Bremner, although you would have thought that Bremner would have been broadly sympathetic to Cook's point of view. They were trying to do the same to me. I was being attacked largely for sexual behaviour, but the motive was political, because of the matters I was trying to raise with the Foreign Office. And on the main issues…the persecution of Muslims, the abuse of human rights for political advantage, Extraordinary Rendition, I've never had a moment's doubt that I'm in the right, and that in time, with the benefit of hindsight, when we recover a balance…a balanced view of these things…people will see I was right… (*Goes.*)

MARGARET: I went back to Edinburgh the next day; I went out to get the papers…what was interesting…the story wasn't as huge as I thought it might be. Campbell was engineering things that during that weekend and the next few days the spotlight fell on something else…Chris Patten…they made a great deal of it to deflect attention away from us.

I was off work for three weeks…it was a turbulent time…loneliness to which there didn't seem to be an end…like pain from a limb I didn't have. I began to be quite frightened…it was a visceral feeling…I was facing the bureaucracy of the Foreign Office; when I tried to contact Robin through the Foreign Office, when there were things that needed to be discussed, they slammed the shutters.

In that consuming loneliness I thought, 'What will make me feel better?' And I thought, 'Possibly writing to the Press, writing in my name, seeing my name being quoted sympathetically.' I wrote a letter to the *Times*. I felt better. I sent it off. Robin's agent…he rang up, and said, 'It's going to be a difficult first day back at work for you…I'll come up and chum you along. We'll have coffee before you go into the hospital'…I thought out of kindness of heart…can't be rude…I didn't want him there, but I let him come…we had coffee, and then went into my office. I just tossed off the fact that I'd written to he *Times*, and there was an instant transformation. He turned into this raging gorilla. He was incredibly angry. He shouted at me… 'You're not doing Robin any good.' The reason he'd come wasn't to help; it was controlling me. I really had to behave as if nothing had happened.

And then Austin Mitchell's wife…she'd come up to see me, said she was writing a book on Westminster women, did I want to write the whole story, about Heathrow and Gaynor and all that. People tried to accuse me of money seeking, revenge-seeking, thought I was scandalmongering. I didn't see myself as the architect of scandal. Aitken and the Hamiltons made their own scandals, and I, of course, was the victim of scandal. It was to do with me restoring

my own reputation. I realised the extent to which I had
been subservient. I so wanted to point out to Robin…'You
know if you had been the consultant haematologist, and I
had been the MP, yours would have been the important
job, and mine would just have been the dilettante thing to
do.' Anyway, it caused an absolute furore. Suddenly all
the aces I'd held were scattered about. It led to Campbell
blackening my name, as being a vengeful woman…you
should have seen the cartoons appearing at the time…
hands splayed out, the fingers tattooed with 'VENGEANCE',
and all these other words…'ANGER', 'FURY', 'RAGE',
'SPITE'…I had this witch's face. So now they had it all…
I was a virago, and every time Robin tried to stand up
for a moral issue they threatened him with ridicule in the
press to keep him 'on message'. Robin and I…all our life
together we had spent climbing the greasy pole to get to
our relative positions, but he certainly never achieved
much of what he wanted to do, because he was constantly
being undermined by scandal. Scandal is a useful weapon.
Fear of scandal is a useful weapon.

*The company sings 'Who Were You With Last Night?' while
MARGARET turns back into SONAL.*

LOUISE: Robin Cook…yeah.

SONAL: Yeah.

LOUISE: Yeah, I've heard of him. He used to be a politician.
I'm pretty sure he had an affair. I think he died.

SONAL: You're thinking of someone else.

LOUISE: No, he died. Aitken? Yes, I have heard that name
Aitken. I can't think why.

SONAL: No.

LOUISE: I have. Brocket? Oh yeah.

SONAL: Yeah… 'I'm a Celebrity, Get Me Out of Here!'…

LOUISE: And something else. The Ingrams? No.

SONAL: No.

LOUISE: Oh, Major Ingram…oh them, course we heard of them.

SONAL: Oh them, yeah…they were on 'Celebrity Wife Swap'.

LOUISE: Yeah. Edwina Currie…she was on 'Celebrity Wife Swap' as well…she had to live with the man who wears a hat in bed…she threw a glass of champagne on him when he was in bed. Wasn't she a politician?

SONAL: I dunno.

LOUISE: I'm sure she was a politician, a long time ago. The Hamiltons? Oh yeah, yeah…course we know them…

SONAL: Everyone knows them.

LOUISE: Didn't they make a Christmas single?

SONAL: They went on 'Who Wants To Be A Millionaire?' for charity, which was really good.

LOUISE: Lord Montagu? No.

SONAL: No.

LOUISE: The Hamiltons…I'm sure they had a scandal. I can't remember what it was. I think he got the sack for it.

SONAL: Everyone likes the Hamiltons.

LOUISE: Christine Hamilton had to live on a roof. If she wanted a bar of soap or a towel she had to get it on the Internet. I was living in Germany at the time, and I remember asking my mum, 'Why does Christine Hamilton have to live on a roof?'

SONAL: They've got their act now.

LOUISE: They must be cleverer than they make out to be, cos they've made money out of it, and people really like them.

SONAL: Yeah.

LOUISE: Weren't they falsely accused of something?

The company sings another verse of 'Who Were You With Last Night?' while LOUISE transforms into CHRISTINE HAMILTON on stage.

CHRISTINE: I've always said we're like Marmite…people either like us or loathe us, but even the people who loathed us knew it was preposterous. Their hearts must have leapt and thought 'Wow', but even they after two seconds would have realised it was complete rubbish, nonsense on stilts. It should all have been stopped in its tracks in half an hour. Of all the things we could have been accused of...rape!

NEIL: Not just I was accused...Christine was accused too. To accuse a woman as part of a conspiracy to rape is unusual.

CHRISTINE: Lots of celebrities are stalked; names are picked up on the Internet; the name Hamilton clicked in her brain and grew into this kind of nonsense.

NEIL: Just gold-digging.

CHRISTINE: It took a time to sink in...I mean obviously we thought this is absurd, and assumed we could quash the whole thing more or less at once.

NEIL: I realised as a lawyer, it depended on the allegations... on what time of day the goings-on were meant to have taken place. What if she'd said 3 AM in the morning?

CHRISTINE: As we thought the thing through, we realised what a god-awful mess we were in.

NEIL: Fortunately she said five in the afternoon and we had an alibi. She alleged she had been held naked on the floor of this house in Ilford, and raped by this chap. I had knelt by her side and done unspeakable things...

CHRISTINE: And I was wearing a blue dress, and knelt over her face trying to do something else unspeakable, which is absurd for a start, because anyone who knows me knows I never wear blue. Red is my colour and always has been. It's almost a trade mark.

NEIL: And this chap who was supposed to have raped her on the floor while we pinned her down was sixty, enormously overweight, a chronic asthmatic, and so arthritic he had to be carried out of his flat when he was arrested. He told the police he could barely stand, let alone kneel.

CHRISTINE: Can you believe it? Within two days of Nadine Milroy-Sloan's complaint, the police had CCTV footage proving they weren't even in this flat in Ilford at the time.

NEIL: And if the Met had bothered to check with the Lincolnshire police, they would have told them she had a record of sexual fantasy, including allegations against her own grandmother. But of course she went to Max Clifford, that's why the story developed.

CHRISTINE: Fortunately we had people round for dinner that evening, so we couldn't have been in two places at once…though this policeman asked me if I'd left my guests for any length of time. 'Oh yes', I told him, 'after the jellied Bloody Marys – one of my specialities – we drove to Ilford, raped somebody, drove back, served the meat and two veg and no one noticed.' Honestly…but it just goes to show how you can become public property.

NEIL: Once you've been scandalised, you're open season.

CHRISTINE: Yes…that phrase…'Just when you thought it was safe to go back in the water.'

CHARLES and DIANA re-enter.

DIANA: There's definitely something. Once you've been convicted in court for something scandalous, you're fair game…wherever you go, whatever you do.

CHARLES: Kick a man while he's down. There are relatively few people who can be poked fun at without any fear of reprisal.

DIANA: Obviously if you go on something like 'The Weakest Link' with Anne Robinson, you know you're going to get a hard time. But any time anything happens…like for instance I had a bump in the car, and I phoned up to make a claim, it takes twice as long, because you have to get it absolutely right…the nuance of every single question… because of what happened on 'Who Wants To Be A Millionaire?', you have to be sure to answer every question absolutely correctly, even when it's an insurance claim.

CHARLES: It's persecution…sheer, unabashed persecution. It only to goes to show we're a nation of curtain-twitchers… like to know what's going on behind other people's curtains while retaining our own privacy.

CHRISTINE: We live on the seventh floor, and at one stage during the Nadine Milroy-Sloan incident, a camera on a cherry-picker...a crane...reared its head at our window, trying to look inside. And the whole fiasco was splashed all over every paper...'Hamiltons on sex charges'.

NEIL: Unlike later when we were proclaimed to be completely innocent.

CHRISTINE: Two lines at the bottom of page nineteen, though that was hardly surprising given it was day after the planes flew into the Twin Towers.

DIANA: For a long time the Press turned up...not every day, but most days...one day two chaps from the *Sun* turned up... 'Is it true Charles was caught cheating during an orienteering exam when he was at Sandhurst? Is it true he took a shortcut from A to B?' I mean isn't that just what you're supposed to do? Orienteering is the quickest way from A to B. Extraordinary...stupid...the things they come up with.

CHRISTINE: How about 'CHRISTINE'S LESBIAN LUST'? After the Nadine Milroy-Sloan incident, the early edition of the *News of the World* printed 'CHRISTINE'S LESBIAN LUST'. It was strip at the top of the paper; they printed it in the early editions. A friend of ours picked it up at the railway station. It was gone by the main edition...they'd thought better of it.

NEIL: We sued them too.

CHRISTINE: Didn't see why they should get away with it.

NEIL: The *News of the World* caved in just like that. It was just part of the production costs.

DIANA: Complete nutters...we get complete nutters on the doorstep...this man arrived one day and knocked on the door...how does he know where we live, that's what I want to know...he said, 'Hello, I was just passing...I'm on my way from Devon to London so I thought I'd just pop by and say hello.' So I said, 'Hello', and he said, 'I saw you on the television the other day, I thought you were marvellous. You're marvellous. I like a stern woman. I like a dominatrix.' He was getting quite excited and then said, 'Must go...sorry...bye.'

CHARLES: One morning I opened the door, and there was this chap...reporter from the *Sunday Express*...you wouldn't pour me another cup of tea would you darling...

DIANA: Oh alright...don't Maggie...how many times...those aren't for you...

CHARLES: He had a photographer with him and asked...

DIANA: (*Pouring tea.*) Honestly, can you believe it?

CHARLES: He asked...

DIANA: He said to Charles, 'Have you ever been in Hyde Park?' He said, 'Yes, of course.' Well of course he's been in Hyde Park...when we're in London, we quite often walk in Hyde Park. And then he asked, 'Do you know any Chinese people?' And of course he knows some Chinese people... well one or two...

CHARLES: Sort of innocent questions which I answered honestly...

DIANA: And there was this huge article...'MAJOR INGRAM IS CHINESE SPY' and 'INGRAM SELLS GOVERNMENT SECRETS TO THE CHINESE' with this story of how he'd been seen shaking hands with these Chinese people in Hyde Park, and a grainy photograph of some people shaking hands, who, actually, could have been anybody...I mean, can you believe it? Absurd.

(*Gives tea.*)

CHARLES: Nobody believes me...nobody. Journalists come, we get on really well; they go away convinced of my innocence...

DIANA: They say they are...

CHARLES: Then when the article comes out, we're completely shafted...that we're either nice people and or innocent is no news. Journalists have got to be as hideous as possible to get the articles printed...so people read their newspaper and not someone else's.

AITKEN returns with another bottle of red wine. DAVID LEIGH enters.

CHRISTINE: There are the endless cheap jibes…laughing at our expense…well, you've just got to learn to live with them, quite frankly. We'd turn up to speak at an event, and the chairman…he could even be the Chairman of the local Rotary Club…but he would introduce us…'Blah blah blah…thrilled to have Neil and Christine Hamilton to speak to us, and their fee will be in the normal brown envelope.' It's not done maliciously.

NEIL: 'A warm welcome to Britain's most notorious couple.'

CHRISTINE: I don't mind that one…I don't mind any of it really.

NEIL: I always get 'Disgraced Tory MP' in some papers.

CHRISTINE: Hit a button and it all comes out.

AITKEN: That's a perennial one for me…disgraced…disgraced Cabinet Minister, former prisoner, ex-jail-bird. There was a time when I was sort of…sort of…felt I was…it was yet another painful thrust of the journalistic dagger into me. But you have to recognise you're raw about these things, and to have a sense of time and patience and your relative unimportance. Ex-jail-bird…so what…it's just a label… perfectly fair. I've made friendly peace with the editor of the *Guardian*. I was invited to a party…

DAVID: When we launched the new size semi-tabloid *Guardian*, Alan Rusbridger had a grand party, and I'm trying to remember…it was some posh spot…may come back to me…and in a gesture of Christian rapprochement, he invited Aitken…as you can imagine I was a bit neutral about that…you can take Christianity too far.

AITKEN: On the whole the people there, after getting over the surprise of seeing me there, were perfectly willing to let bygones be bygones…but there was this one man, David Leigh…he made the World in Action programme, 'Jonathan of Arabia', and was I suppose the protagonist at the *Guardian*…he was strange…it's still clear, even after all this time…he's got a…got strong personal feelings…wasn't prepared to let bygones be bygones…

DAVID: Yes, I'm David Leigh. My wife, Jeannie, she's a barrister, she was at the party with me…she saw Jonno there, and was consumed with fury…marched up to him and gave him what-for. I was lurking in the corner. I'm easily embarrassed, I don't like scenes; I grew up in Nottingham; we don't do scenes in Nottingham. Jeannie denounced him vigorously, perhaps inappropriately, over how he'd made my life a misery, and how a friend of his at the trial had described *Guardian* journalists as ugly and stunted with bedraggled wives. I have to say I wasn't very keen to converse with him…his protestations of a Christian family life just make me laugh…he was horrible sexually… horrible…

AITKEN: Yes, I am a bit ashamed of all that, and it's in the past now, but I was a little surprised to have the first stones cast by the impeccable paragons of the *Guardian*.

DAVID: But you're not getting objectivity from me…waving his Sword of Truth and screaming at me, Aitken had ratcheted the stakes up so high, one of us would have to be destroyed.

AITKEN: Whatever you've done wrong, and I've done plenty, the number one priority is genuine repentance…an acceptance that you and you alone have cocked your life up. What you can't do is be like Caliban and rage at yourself in the glass, or like Prospero…going over and over the events that led to your downfall, hoping that this time they'll turn out right. Magic reversals of fortune? No. You've got to flush all those ideas down the loo and then absolutely look at yourself in the mirror, look at yourself…

DAVID: When Aitken looks in the mirror, he sees something he wants to see.

AITKEN: And say to yourself, 'You are the master architect and engineer of your own destruction.' Don't waste time in blaming the deckhands and sub-lieutenants. The buck stops with you. Sorry, mixing my metaphors tonight.

DAVID: Aitken's God tells him what he wants to hear. Now everything's going to be fine, and you're redeemed. Aitken found a way of forgiving himself, which is unconvincing to me...I may be jaundiced.

AITKEN: The past is another country...you've got to move on.

DAVID: Why I don't buy his Christian remorse was that he tried to get his old seat back when he came out of prison. If he felt an ounce of genuine remorse, he wouldn't dream of going back into politics. I don't think he's confronted his crimes; I think he's rewritten the script. Surely if you feel real remorse you dig your garden, go shopping for old ladies, and duck out of the public eye. If he had any proper humility he would keep his head down and say to himself, 'I am after all a criminal. I'm not a wise man, I'm a foolish man.' He's not willing to accept being a nobody; he's trying to get back that feeling of entitlement. And I would say to him, 'You're not entitled to anything; you're a crooked liar.'

The classic case of how to do it right is Profumo...he went to such extraordinary lengths to rehabilitate himself... doing good works forever. Certainly he's held in the public mind as having achieved a state of grace through expiation. At the other end of the scale you have Jeffrey Archer, rolling in money, armoured in self-delusion, invincibly self-confident, and unable to separate truth from fiction in his own mind...but what do I know? I'm just phrase-making.

AITKEN: The biggest hurdle I would say is cutting your own ego down to size. If other people try to do the surgery it doesn't work...it has to be you.

DAVID: All my targets have been grandiose; they all took a punt on fame, all think they could have been Prime Minister. If I've stopped them from being Prime Minister, I've helped in a small way, and saved the commonwealth from a grizzly fate. If they put their lives together again, that absolves me from guilt...I can sleep again.

I do genuinely admire Jonno for putting his life back together again...it shows strength of character...he could have collapsed. But I still feel ambivalent about inviting him to the *Guardian* re-launch party. The Hamiltons...the real problem with them...any probation officer will tell you...if you're not going to confront your crimes, you're not going to be rehabilitated. Christine's the one I admire...you can't help admiring her resilience...you'd want to bottle that and sell it, wouldn't you?

NEIL: I think David Leigh should be bottled...how I'll leave to your fecund imagination.

CHRISTINE: His horrible face...

NEIL: In formaldehyde preferably.

CHRISTINE: I think he must have modelled for Hieronymous Bosch.

DAVID: As long as they're impervious, they have no chance of spiritual recovery...if you haven't confronted the reality, there's no way back into public life. This appears to be the bill; this is the price to pay, thank you waiter. As long as you quibble about the bill...'The wine wasn't this much...I didn't have the calamari'...then you never get to leave the restaurant, do you? But they're all frightfully resilient, like cockroaches after the nuclear holocaust...there they all are crawling around, waving their little feelers, indestructibly.

DAVID leaves and changes into BROCKET.

The rest of the company enters and sings one verse of 'Pick Yourself Up, Dust Yourself Off, Start All Over Again'.

CHRISTINE: Neil and I had always said, 'No, we're not going abroad, we're not slinking off, there's no reason to hide under a stone. Neil...which wallah is ours, do you remember?

NEIL: That one I think.

CHRISTINE: Grab his attention next time he passes...I need some more hot water. Sometimes when I look back now, I wonder how we did it. People have no idea of the turmoil underneath...actually I think 'turmoil beneath' would be more playwrighterly.

BROCKET: My Irish heritage, fortunately or unfortunately, is very strong in me…it leads to an irritating sense of humour, which my father certainly had until he died of his brain tumour. And it's that gets you through the bad times. You get a setback today; when you look back in a year or two years' time, you think, 'Thank God that happened; it caused a change of direction.'

AITKEN: You know I sometimes say in my prayers, 'Thank you God for sending me to prison' because without going through the depths of defeat, disgrace, divorce, bankruptcy, and gaol, I wouldn't have started to change direction and begun a spiritual journey.

BROCKET: There's an upside…you see I really do believe there's a reason for everything…except parking tickets… they irritate the shit out of me.

AITKEN: It was the engine of pride that got me into the 'Unsheathing of the Sword of Truth' speech…stupid and silly pride. Why did I ever tell a lie in the first place? I was afraid of being humiliated by the newspapers. You start to fight on their territory, but what I've learned is that their territory and my territory is a rather meaningless battleground.

BROCKET: If you don't believe there's an upside, you're a miserable old sod, and you might as well lock yourself away as a recluse.

NEIL: We weren't just going to lie down and be steamrollered by all and sundry.

CHRISTINE: (*To WAITER.*) Could I have some more hot water please? What about you Neil?

NEIL: I'll have another pot of Earl Grey please…that's lemon not milk, thanks so much.

WAITER: One pot of Earl Grey, one hot water.

NEIL: We scratched a living, charged for any and every TV and radio interview…twenty-four pounds or thirty-two pounds I think for a radio interview.

CHRISTINE: We did what any other unemployed couple would do.

NEIL: Cancelled all newspapers and magazines.

CHRISTINE: Never to be resurrected I'm pleased to say.

NEIL: Selling little bits of china at fairs. I had my parliamentary gratuity but no work, and no prospect of work.

CHRISTINE: It was a jolly tough fight. I suppose I thought, 'I'm not going to have the rest of my life wrecked by an Egyptian grocer.' We did things on telly...stupid games shows.

NEIL: We were treated as a freak show.

CHRISTINE: We had to endure being treated as a freak show; and we've gone on from there really...cheesy biscuits, fishnet tights...

NEIL: Pantomime in Guildford.

CHRISTINE: A lot of people thought, 'How low can you get?' but we held our own.

MONTAGU comes on with a copy of his autobiography.

MONTAGU: I was determined not to run away. Sadder and wiser, but I wasn't ashamed.

NEIL: Had to bite our lip and get on with it.

MONTAGU: The first thing I had to face was the home situation...meeting the neighbours...the Beaulieu Estate is quite large...a lot of people living on it...and the staff of course. You would be inspecting a farm building being repaired, that sort of thing, and projecting onto them, 'Oh God, what might they be thinking?'...some of them anyway. The first meeting was apprehensive...some did look you in the face, some didn't. Second time it was fine, it faded away...didn't seem to matter.

CHRISTINE: Over the years, people have more or less forgotten how and why we were catapulted into the limelight.

BROCKET: Yes, the public have changed their attitude towards me...like the fact I'm straight about things... 'Charlie doesn't say things how they should be; he says it how they are.' And the average guy in the street's starting to say, 'Who gives a shit? There's no sex involved, he didn't take anything', and they see all these banks and corporations as the bad guys anyway...they're always shafting us...so 'Good on you mate' is the attitude.

CHRISTINE: People now say, 'I don't really care...sod it...I like you as people.'

NEIL: Yes, I admit...I hanker after something more intellectually stimulating than throwing custard pies around. Cheering the country up...that's our job. We've made ourselves a pair of Butlin's Redcoats to the nation. It's unlikely my professional skills as a politician will ever be put to good use again. I'm in the dustbin of history, where all the others will be shortly...although I keep my hand in as a lawyer... every year I take on a number of pro bono cases...people who can't afford lawyers, but are being treated unjustly.

CHRISTINE: That to me is the tragedy of the whole thing... since the age of twelve, thirteen...his entire hopes and dreams were set on politics.

NEIL: If things had turned out differently, it might have been me rather than Iain Duncan Smith who became leader of the party.

CHRISTINE: Those dreams have been shattered. That's what's so awful. In a curious way, the whole thing has put me on the map. I think I'm happier as a media butterfly. (*Mobile phone goes.*) Excuse me. (*She chats away sotto voce over the next minute or so.*)

NEIL: I'm more like a media caterpillar.

CHARLES: What keeps us going?

DIANA: Our children really. Keeping the family together... making sure our three children are well rounded and well educated.

CHARLES: I'll bullet-point it for you. I'm not going to put these in any order of priority. Firstly, the children; secondly, a deep sense of injustice, which means proving my innocence. I definitely want to re-establish my integrity and that doesn't mean mud-wrestling with the Hamiltons, which we were asked to do on the 'Harry Hill Show'.

DIANA: It wasn't mud-wrestling, it was ordinary fighting.

CHARLES: Oh, I thought it was mud-wrestling.

DIANA: It was fighting, ordinary fighting in a ring.

CHARLES: And thirdly, a love for my country, yet a fear for where it's going; and the mere fact that we have to put food on the table, and a roof over our heads.

DIANA: And our love for each other.

CHARLES: And our love for each other.

DIANA: We always hope there's something round the corner, don't we?

CHARLES: Oh yes, it's not over yet.

CHARLES and DIANA go.

CHRISTINE: (*Switching off phone.*) That was *Closer* magazine... they do a column every week called 'Talking Point'. It's not that deep...celebrity trivia mainly...I've done it several times. This week's topic is, 'Men are better liars than women'. I'm not going to touch that with a bargepole, because of the hinterland. Well I might. I'm busy this week. I'm doing two or three slots a week on 'This Morning'... I'm doing five different programmes about 'I'm a Celebrity, Get Me Out of Here!'...studio commentary and analysis. I write an article for a Scottish newspaper. Friday I'm getting up at God knows what hour...I'm reviewing the papers for 'News 24'. Don't knock it...it pays the bills.

NEIL: We have a lot of student fans; we're popular amongst blacks.

CHRISTINE: I'm a gay icon, which is very nice. 'I'm a Celebrity, Get Me Out of Here!' did a lot to help our general credibility.

BROCKET: The turning point for me was 'I'm a Celebrity, Get Me Out of Here!'. I thought I was going to win...

Ladbrokes thought so anyway, until I called Jenny Bond an old slapper...that rather did for me.

CHRISTINE: When I came out of the jungle, people said, 'Shock, horror, she's normal, just like the rest of us.' That's all we've done really...gone on being ourselves.

NEIL: We haven't changed...it's other people's perception of us that has changed.

BROCKET: What was quite interesting was the upper classes, people from my background and level...I went up to the Duke of Buccleuch's place in the Scottish Borders...and I'd just come out of the jungle six months before...it was a big charity lunch...and there were a fair number of Dukes dotted around the lunch table, and this seriously aristocratic chap came towards me, and I thought, 'Wait for it, here it comes...a metaphorical slap in the face' you know...and he said, 'What we saw in the jungle, the way you conducted yourself, and the way you represented our class, has done our class proud. You have done more to help the image of the aristocracy than anyone else has done in decades.' And the people around applauded and said, 'Here here.'

MONTAGU: Yes, there was a moment...when I got married in 1959...at Beaulieu in the church next to the house. It didn't pour with rain, a little rain perhaps...as I came out of the church after the wedding...that was the moment...I thought, 'Ah, back to normal.' Well, not normal, life can never be the same after scandal...but as good as it could be in the circumstances. Yes, pick yourself up, dust yourself off...absolutely...

CHRISTINE: And we've bought this house. It's an 'up-yours' house certainly. Quirky, rambling and romantic...a bit like Neil.

NEIL: We should have called it 'Two Fingers'.

CHRISTINE: And we bought it through luck, hard work, sheer bloody-mindedness, and reality TV.

NEIL: Some of it's medieval...around 1400...

CHRISTINE: We hoped it would give Fayed terminal heart failure. It didn't unfortunately, but it undoubtedly caused his heart to skip a few beats. He was apoplectic...it was wonderful. Neil, can you remember what the grocer said when we bought our house?

NEIL: 'Life is unfair.'

CHRISTINE: 'Life is unfair.' How disgraceful.

BROCKET: Life is fun now. The Ferraris have all been reassembled and are back on the road. I said to my agent I'll take this year off...we're buying a house in France, the kids have come back from South America; I'll do the odd bit of writing and photography, write the odd political bit if someone's pissing the shit out of me. Yeah, it's a long way from the dark days of prison. (*Goes.*)

MONTAGU: Looking back now, I could state quite definitely that my prison experience did me good. It made me concentrate on what mattered most...stately homes, old cars, jazz festivals, President of the Historic Houses Association, English Heritage, and indeed prison reform.

EDWINA: After I turned down the prisons offer, my agent took me out to lunch, and said, 'If Jeffrey Archer can write a novel, you can write a novel.' I wrote a synopsis about 4 MPs and a would-be MP at a crisis point in the life of each character...it was all about rape, betrayal and blackmail...I thought it might as well be about exciting stuff...I steeled myself to write the sex scenes. It was in the top ten for ten weeks.

MONTAGU: I would like to think my achievements have outstripped my shortcomings. And I don't mind being quoted on this...our case...us three...did more to change the law on homosexuality than any other incident.

EDWINA: About that time I was asked to front up the gay rights campaign to lower the age of consent...I thought, 'Yup, I agree with that.' When it came to the Parliamentary debate, and the age went down from twenty-one to eighteen...the next morning...I came to go to my office... I turned the corner, and the flowers stretched all the way down the corridor. My secretary asked, 'What shall I do with all these?' I said, 'Send them across the river to St Thomas's.' That morning...it was the first time for a long time that I had felt loved.

MONTAGU: I like to think it was our attitude, our behaviour during the proceedings and during our prison sentences. And being constructive, and not cashing in; I was offered twenty thousand pounds by the *Sunday Despatch* for the story...I turned it down. Yes, I'm proud of it now.

EDWINA: At the next election we didn't just lose we were wiped...whole areas of the country without a Tory MP. I lost my seat. I'd split up with my husband...it happened very quietly...no one noticed. I'm good at keeping things quiet. I had my late-night phone-in on the BBC. I was living fairly frugally.

In 1999, John Major brought out his autobiography to general acclaim. Everyone said, 'What a good guy. This mess the Tory Party's in is really nothing to do with the last government; John Major wasn't responsible.' I said, 'Oh yes he fucking well was.' He sought the job when he was incapable of doing it...he was dreadfully weak in office, procrastinating, petty, small-minded, vacillating...failed to grasp events, failed to lead. More than that...he came up with phrases like, 'I believe in instincts, not experts.' He was no good at maths, he didn't understand the statistics, that's why he said 'I trust my instincts.' 'You're running the country for God's sake.' Way, way, way out of his depth. And I thought to myself, 'The time is coming when I will say something and why.'

In 2001 I had met and married Mr Jones, and he's an absolute winner. If you watched 'Celebrity Wife Swap' you'll have seen he's thoughtful, original and kind. I talked the whole thing through with him. I said, 'Mr John Major's been whitewashed as a secular saint, which he ain't, and the time has come to tell the story.' And I began to think, 'I'm not going to be airbrushed out of history, and I shouldn't go on protecting this extremely strange man longer than I think is necessary. I'm going to put the record straight, in as simple and unadorned fashion as possible from notes I made at the time. The truth will out, and I will be the architect of that truth.'

MONTAGU: I wanted to tell my own story in my own way, not let someone else do it. I've got a copy of my book for you to read.

CHRISTINE: Have you read my book? I think you'd enjoy it.

NEIL: It's a very good read.

CHRISTINE: Thank you darling. It is a good read. A bit chatty, a bit *Mail on Sunday*, you know, but it is a good read. Anyway come on Neil, we'd better be off. We're driving down to Wiltshire tonight.

NEIL: Yes, thanks for the tea. It's been very nice to meet you.

CHRISTINE: It has. It's been fun.

The HAMILTONS leave.

MONTAGU: When I came to write my book, I was looking at the records of the court cases and the newspaper reports of the time.

EDWINA: When it all happened, I was writing a lot…the words were pouring out of me…I was pouring my whole self into the records I was creating.

MONTAGU: They'd been kept in a bank, locked away in a bank for fifty years…no one had looked at them for fifty years, and suddenly there I was reading them again. It brought it all back…you can imagine…it was quite traumatic.

EDWINA: People didn't see that I was analysing weakness… was making a political analysis. They saw it in the light of, 'Wicked woman tells all about a man who should have known better.' Still, from the perspective of now, I've rewritten history. I don't see it as scandal. I think it's important to get the details right, to pass on history as correctly as possible. I've achieved that. He's now in the public estimate where he ought to be. No, no…I've won.

A male FLOOR MANAGER hurries on.

FLOOR MANAGER: I hope I'm not interrupting…I've got a rather anxious editor upstairs saying, 'Is Edwina here?', and I said, 'I think I've spotted her.' Sorry if I'm interrupting…he's getting a bit anxious…he says Edwina's on air in six minutes.

EDWINA: Must go…thanks for lunch…keep in touch. (*Goes.*)

MENAJI: I'm in the West End, standing outside a hotel… waiting for Chantelle, who may or may not arrive. Fucking cold. She's got married today, and we've had a tip-off that she may be coming here for the reception. It might be a false trail…the info comes from anywhere…somewhere in the PR…friends, family. I've been here two hours already, and I'm feeling a bit negged out. Even if we get the photographs, *OK* may buy them off us so they keep the exclusive…they've got the exclusive on the wedding photos…that's what makes me think it's disinformation. There are only four of us here, so we would do a split anyway…make it an exclusive for one of us, and divide the money four ways…it's better than flogging it all round the papers. I only hope the cow turns up, or else I'm wasting my fucking time.

MONTAGU: I did tell my son…he was…I told both my sons in fact…ten years apart. They couldn't have cared less. I wanted them to know. The one thing that worries me now is that it's going to remind the family of something that they've forgotten.

DAVID: I would say Montagu was a victim of primitive social attitudes, and shouldn't have been scandalised in the way he was, or indeed punished in the way he was.

AITKEN: I've known Montagu on and off for a number of years. There was an Annual General Meeting of an admirable organisation called the New Bridge Society…it builds bridges to help ex-offenders back into society. Almost as I was coming in, there was a man in his seventies coming out, and this was Montagu. We crossed at the back of the hall, and there were people on the platform speaking, so we couldn't have a chat and...but...our eyes met. I suddenly realised, he suddenly realised...there we were, two wounded birds, two members of the bruised pilgrims club, and we couldn't say anything which made it all the more poignant...we just had time to look each other in the eye, shake hands and move on.

DAVID: The whole scenario is difficult...horribly difficult... how if I was dragged into the limelight, and things I'm ashamed of were dragged into the public domain...think how horribly traumatised I would be. I often think, 'Thank God I'm ordinary.'

AITKEN: We over-punish our public figures for their transgressions. We make them into idols wrongly. We puff them up wrongly. We drag them earthwards wrongly. We abuse them wrongly. We give scandal too great a credence. We demean ourselves by going to the level of the people who peddle in scandal. (*Goes.*)

DAVID: These cases where people in the public eye are elevated and then dragged down and torn to pieces by the crowd are all theatre...a rather unpleasant form of theatre. That's what the Max Cliffords of this world understand. They aren't driven by anything except a desire to make money, and exude nothing but a slimy hypocrisy. That's what they do...they stage these performances. Act One. Here is a celebrity to admire, fawn over, gawp at. Act Two. Get the celebrity into trouble, and start dragging them down. Act Three. Trample the celebrity into the mud to make you feel better about the feelings of envy stirred up by your initial adoration.

MENAJI: No...she never turned up...Chantelle. It's totally negged me out. Waste of life, waste of space. The husband and wifey went off somewhere else for an *OK* exclusive... some of the family turned up here, but they brought a hundred other photographers with them, so there was no value in it at all. Pathetic bollocks...wasting my fucking life. Sometimes I get caught up in the negativity of it all. All we do is slag people off. There must be a better way. I might as well be photographing a cum shot in a porno movie. It's all about ignorance and selfishness. Life's a bitch.

DAVID: It's a horrible, moronic catharsis…a theatre for morons. Everyone comes and pisses on your grave; gnaws bits off you. It doesn't matter if the actors are good or bad…it's just a tragic-comic role they've been required to play. The nasty cynical Rupert Murdochs of this world understand this…and they just make enormous sums of money out of our pathological attitudes.

MENAJI: What's wrong with everybody? They're all focused on bollocks. No one's telling the truth. You need discrimination, values, dignity. It's about staying free and not getting caught up in the system. Knowledge is not imprisoning ourselves with limited thinking…and that's what scandal is…limited thinking. You must see how easy it is to manipulate people with it, cos their lives are so thin, because they want to concentrate on what's juicy, dodgy and dark…cos we're so fucking lost…dodgy, dark, and negative.

The company sing a blues version of 'Pick Yourself Up, Dust Yourself Off, Start All Over Again'. EDWARD MONTAGU makes his way slowly to the front of the stage.

MONTAGU: I was determined to implant in the public consciousness something more important than my going to prison. Gradually I hoped that what the public would come to associate me with was a motor museum, not boy scouts…jazz and historic houses, not airmen. Have I succeeded? I rather think that's for you to say, not me.

He turns and slowly walks off as the company finish the song.

Blackout.